lonely planet

W9-BZT-950

Pocket

MELBOURNE

TOP SIGHTS • LOCAL LIFE • MADE EASY

Kate Morgan, Cristian Bonetto, Peter Dragicevich

In This Book

QuickStart Guide

Your keys to understanding the city – we help you decide what to do and how to do it

Need to Know
Tips for a smooth trip

Neighbourhoods
What's where

Explore Melbourne

The best things to see and do, neighbourhood by neighbourhood

Top Sights
Make the most of your visit

Local Life
The insider's city

The Best of Melbourne

The city's highlights in handy lists to help you plan

Best Walks
See the city on foot

Melbourne's Best...
The best experiences

Survival Guide

Tips and tricks for a seamless, hassle-free city experience

Getting Around
Travel like a local

Essential Information
Including where to stay

Our selection of Melbourne's best places to eat, drink and experience:

◎ **Sights**

✖ **Eating**

☕ **Drinking**

✪ **Entertainment**

🔒 **Shopping**

These symbols give you the vital information for each listing:

☏ Telephone Numbers	✤ Family-Friendly
⊙ Opening Hours	🐾 Pet-Friendly
P Parking	🚍 Bus
⊘ Nonsmoking	⛴ Ferry
@ Internet Access	M Metro
🛜 Wi-Fi Access	S Subway
🥗 Vegetarian Selection	🚊 Tram
📖 English-Language Menu	🚆 Train

Find each listing quickly on maps for each neighbourhood:

Bar Hemingway

16 ☕ Map p233, B2

Legend has it that Hem self, wielding a machine rate this timber-pan ered bar during showpiece is a n by Papa ar town. Dress s.com; Hôtel Rit ⊙6.30pm-2a

16 ☕

6 ◎ Plac

Lonely Planet's Melbourne

Lonely Planet Pocket Guides are designed to get you straight to the heart of the city.

Inside you'll find all the must-see sights, plus tips to make your visit to each one really memorable. We've split the city into easy-to-navigate neighbourhoods and provided clear maps so you'll find your way around with ease. Our expert authors have searched out the best of the city: walks, food, nightlife and shopping, to name a few. Because you want to explore, our 'Local Life' pages will take you to some of the most exciting areas to experience the real Melbourne.

And of course you'll find all the practical tips you need for a smooth trip: itineraries for short visits, how to get around, and how much to tip the guy who serves you a drink at the end of a long day's exploration.

It's your guarantee of a really great experience.

Our Promise

You can trust our travel information because Lonely Planet authors visit the places we write about, each and every edition. We never accept freebies for positive coverage, so you can rely on us to tell it like it is.

QuickStart Guide   7

Explore Melbourne   21

Worth a Trip:

The Best of Melbourne 153

Melbourne's Best Walks

Melbourne's Best...

Survival Guide 175

QuickStart Guide

Welcome to Melbourne

Stylish, arty Melbourne is both dynamic and cosmopolitan, and it's proud of its place as Australia's sporting and cultural capital. Stately architecture and a multicultural make-up reflect the city's history, while street art and sticky-carpeted venues point to its present-day personality. It's also a top sporting city, playing host to Grand Slam tennis, Formula One and – its main obsession – Aussie Rules footy.

Hosier Lane (p34)
PATJO/SHUTTERSTOCK ©

Melbourne
Top Sights

Federation Square
(p24)

The city's epicentre with top galleries

Royal Botanic
Gardens (p74)

Melbourne's world-famous green lung

NGV International
(p50)

Impressive collection of artwork spanning the globe

St Kilda Foreshore
(p140)

Sea breezes and lively nightlife

Melbourne Museum (p122)

Victoria's natural and cultural histories

Birrarung Marr (p26)

A tranquil tribute to the Indigenous Wurundjeri people

Queen Victoria Market (p28)

Historical market with gourmet produce

Royal Exhibition Building (p124)

Melbourne's only Unesco World Heritage Site

Melbourne Cricket Ground (p90)
Hallowed turn for sporting fans

Abbotsford Convent (p118)
Hub of artistic activity in a former convent

Melbourne
Local Life

*Local experiences and hidden gems
to help you uncover the real city*

After checking out Melbourne's top sights, here's how you can experience what makes the city tick – cool city laneways, a thriving live-music scene, hip inner-city suburbs, local designers, and an obsession with great coffee and craft breweries.

Arcades & Laneways (p30)
☑ Street art ☑ Laneway bars

Williamstown (p60)
☑ Maritime ambience ☑ Science museum

East Brunswick (p100)
☑ Cafes ☑ Local hang-outs

Other great places to experience the city like a local:

Fitzroy & Collingwood Pub Crawl (p104)
☑ Bars and pubs ☑ Late-night eats

Melbourne
Day Planner

Day One

Start at **Federation Square** (p24) and spend the morning exploring the **Ian Potter Centre: NGV Australia** (p34), the **Australian Centre for the Moving Image** (p25) and the **Koorie Heritage Trust** (p35). Wander across Flinders St to **Hosier Lane** (p34) to browse some of Melbourne's most prominent street art. Tuck into tapas at **MoVida** (p40) for lunch.

From Bourke St, jump on a tram heading north to Carlton. Have a good gawk at the World Heritage–listed **Royal Exhibition Building** (p124) before delving into the **Melbourne Museum** (p122). Finish up with a stroll along Lygon St to soak up the old-school Melbourne Italian vibe. Drop into **D.O.C Espresso** (p130) or **Brunetti** (p132) for coffee and cake. For dinner, head back into the city to **Lee Ho Fook** (p37).

While leaving the restaurant, check out the street art on Duckboard Pl before ducking into the **Garden State Hotel** (p44) for a drink. Head around the corner onto AC/DC Lane for more street art and a hard-rock fix at **Cherry** (p31) bar. If you're not finished yet, there are further hip drinking options on and around Flinders Lane.

Day Two

Begin your day at **Queen Victoria Market** (p28), then grab a takeaway flat white at **Market Lane Coffee** (p44) and take a stroll through **Flagstaff Gardens**. Wander up to Flagstaff station and take a train to Jolimont station. Walk up Bridge Rd for a lunch pit stop at **Richmond Hill Cafe & Larder** (p94).

Backtrack down Bridge Rd, turn left onto Punt Rd and then cut across Yarra Park to the **Melbourne Cricket Ground** (p90). If you're a sports fan, join a tour or delve directly into the National Sports Museum. Continue on to **Fitzroy Gardens** (p93) and seek out the Conservatory, Cooks' Cottage, Fairies Tree and miniature Tudor Village. Book into **Cutler & Co** (p108) for Fitzroy fine dining later.

Pop into neighbouring **Marion** (p112) for a wine before dinner. After eating, either call into the **Workers Club** (p115) to see if there's a band playing, or wander along Gertrude St for a cocktail at the **Everleigh** (p112).

Short on time?
We've arranged Melbourne's must-sees into these day-by-day itineraries to make sure you see the very best of the city in the time you have available.

Day Three

Start your day with a walk around the **Royal Botanic Gardens** (p74) and a visit to the **Shrine of Remembrance** (p78). Catch a tram to South Yarra and window-shop along Chapel St and Commercial Rd before calling into **Prahran Market** (p81). Continue the shopping spree on Greville St and then continue up Chapel St to Windsor. Head up to the rooftop at **Fonda** (p81) for a Mexican meal.

Jump on a tram to spend the afternoon in St Kilda. Enjoy sea breezes along its picturesque **foreshore** (p140), look for little penguins on the pier, stop for a drink with a view at the pier kiosk and check out Luna Park. Those who like to mix drinking with leisurely activities should head to the **St Kilda Bowling Club** (p149). Sit down for a seafood feast at **Stokehouse** (p145) or the more casual **Pontoon** (p149) downstairs.

If there's nothing on at the nearby **Palais Theatre** (p141), head on to **Republica** (p149) for a drink with the local larrikins. From here continue along The Esplanade and onto Fitzroy St to throw yourself into St Kilda's notorious nightlife.

Day Four

Devote a large chunk of your morning to exploring the extraordinary art at the **NGV International** (p50). Call into **Arts Centre Melbourne** (p53) to see what's on and then take a stroll along the river. Indulge in a lengthy yum cha session at **Spice Temple** (p54).

Hop on a ferry to Williamstown to get a different perspective of the Yarra. Take a walk along the lovely promenade to **Williamstown Beach** (p61) for a quick dip, otherwise spend time at **Scienceworks** (p61) or check out **HMAS Castlemaine** (p61), a WWII minesweeper.

Catch the train to Parliament station and spend the evening exploring rooftop and laneway bars. Start by rooftop-hopping from **Siglo** (p42) to **Madame Brussels** (p42). Make your way down the murky back alley to the fabulously creepy **Croft Institute** (p42). Get a rock fix at **Heartbreaker** (p42) and grab a whisky nightcap at **Boilermaker House** (p43).

Need to Know

For more information, see Survival Guide (p175)

Currency
Australian Dollars ($)

Language
English

Visas
All visitors, aside from New Zealanders, need a visa to visit Australia. ETA or eVisitor visas can be applied for online at www.border.gov. au; each allow a three-month stay.

Money
ATMs can be found everywhere, and credit cards are widely accepted.

Mobile Phones
Australia's digital network is compatible with GSM 900 and 1800 handsets. Quad-based US phones will also work. Local SIM cards are readily available.

Time
Melbourne is on GMT+10; during daylight savings (late October to late March), Melbourne is 11 hours ahead of GMT.

Plugs & Adaptors
Standard voltage is 240V/50Hz. Plugs are either two-or-three pins. International adaptors are widely available.

Tipping
Not obligatory but around 10% is standard in city restaurants and cafes and is appreciated in bars.

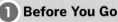 Before You Go

Your Daily Budget

Budget: Less than $200
▶ Dorm bed: $23–40
▶ Pizza, pasta or burger: $7–17
▶ Central-city trams: free

Midrange: $200–320
▶ Double room in a hotel: $130–250
▶ Cafe lunch: $10–30
▶ Public transport: $8.20

Top End: More than $320
▶ Luxury hotel room: $250–1000
▶ Top restaurant meal: $120–350
▶ Tickets to Australian Open men's final: $410–660

Useful Websites

Lonely Planet (www.lonelyplanet.com/melbourne) Destination info, hotel bookings, traveller forum and more.

Broadsheet (www.broadsheet.com.au) Bar, cafe and restaurant reviews.

Visit Melbourne (www.visitmelbourne.com) Events, attractions, travel info.

Advance Planning

Three months before Book your hotel during main events.

One month before Book hostel rooms during summer; high-end restaurants; tickets for international bands.

A few days before Book tickets for local sports events and bands.

② Arriving in Melbourne

Most international and domestic visitors arrive at Tullamarine Airport. Avalon Airport is also used for domestic flights, so check your ticket carefully. Southern Cross Station is a main hub for long-distance trains and buses.

✈ From Melbourne (Tullaramarine) Airport

Destination	Best Transport
Southern Cross Station	SkyBus (☏ 1300 759 287; www.skybus.com.au; Southern Cross station, 99 Spencer St; adult/child $18/9; 🚉 Southern Cross) departs regularly and connects the airport to Southern Cross station 24 hours a day.
City centre	taxis from $50; around 20min

✈ From Avalon Airport

Destination	Best Transport
Southern Cross Station	SkyBus offers a direct bus service
City centre	taxis from $80; 45min to one hour

🚆 From Southern Cross Station

Destination	Best Transport
City centre	train to Flinders Street Station
St Kilda	tram 96 & 12; taxis $25, around 20-30min
Fitzroy/ Collingwood	tram 86 & 11; taxis $20, around 20min

③ Getting Around

Melbourne is well connected by a network of trains, trams and buses operated by Public Transport Victoria (www.ptv.vic.gov.au). Ticketing is through the plastic myki card ($6), a 'touch on, touch off' system, which you put credit on before you travel. Purchase cards at major train stations and 7-Elevens.

🚊 Tram

An extensive network of tramlines runs north–south and east–west along most major roads. Trams run roughly every 10 minutes during the day (more frequently in peak periods), and every 20 minutes in the evening. Trams run until midnight Sunday to Thursday, 1am Friday and Saturday, and six lines run all night on weekends.

🚆 Train

Flinders Street Station is the main metro train station connecting the city and suburbs. The City Loop runs under the city, linking the four corners of town.

🚌 Bus

Melbourne Visitor Shuttle (www.thats melbourne.com.au) visits all the city sights.

🚲 Bicycle

Cycling maps are available from the Melbourne Visitor Centre (www.melbourne.vic. gov.au/touristinformation) at Federation Square and Bicycle Victoria (www.bv.com.au). For short trips, Melbourne Bike Share (www. melbournebikeshare.com.au) offers free 30-minute use of bicycles in the city area, though you need to buy a $5 safety helmet from a 7-Eleven store.

🚕 Taxi

Melbourne's metered taxis are reasonably priced. They require an estimated prepaid fare when hailed between 10pm and 5am.

Melbourne
Neighbourhoods

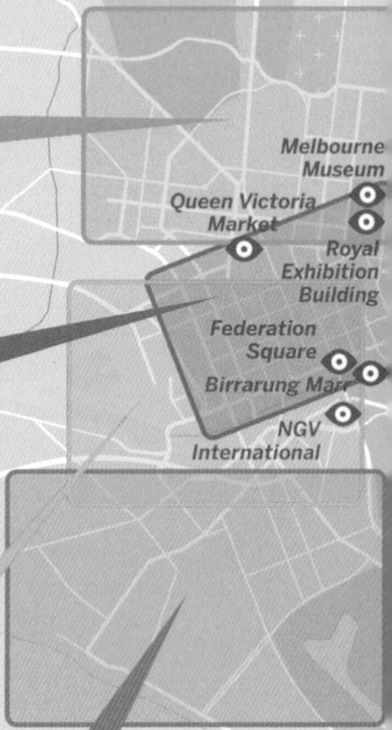

Carlton & Around (p120)
Home to Melbourne's Italian community, mixed in with students, a literary flavour and some outstanding sights.

◉ Top Sights

Melbourne Museum

Royal Exhibition Building

City Centre (p22)
A lively mix of laneways, cool bars and top-notch restaurants, the city's fashionable streets are balanced with pockets of greenery and the Yarra.

◉ Top Sights

Federation Square

Birrarung Marr

Queen Victoria Market

Southbank & Docklands (p48)
Southbank is a slice of European chic along the Yarra. The Docklands is a work in progress, but new eateries make it worth exploring.

◉ Top Sights

NGV International

South Melbourne, Port Melbourne & Albert Park (p62)
Bayside suburbs with a community proud of their local businesses, and the sparkling lake that's home to the Australian Grand Prix.

Melbourne Museum

Queen Victoria Market

Royal Exhibition Building

Federation Square

Birrarung Marr

NGV International

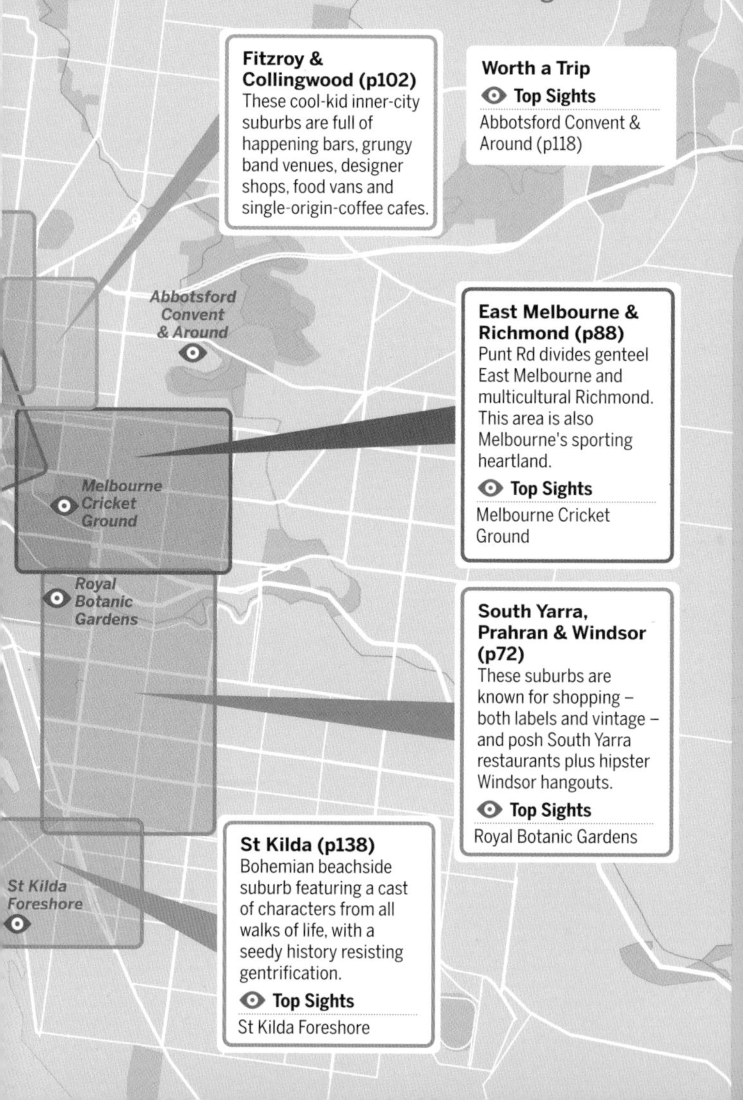

Fitzroy & Collingwood (p102)

These cool-kid inner-city suburbs are full of happening bars, grungy band venues, designer shops, food vans and single-origin-coffee cafes.

Worth a Trip

⊙ Top Sights

Abbotsford Convent & Around (p118)

Abbotsford Convent & Around ⊙

East Melbourne & Richmond (p88)

Punt Rd divides genteel East Melbourne and multicultural Richmond. This area is also Melbourne's sporting heartland.

⊙ Top Sights

Melbourne Cricket Ground

Melbourne Cricket Ground ⊙

Royal Botanic Gardens ⊙

South Yarra, Prahran & Windsor (p72)

These suburbs are known for shopping – both labels and vintage – and posh South Yarra restaurants plus hipster Windsor hangouts.

⊙ Top Sights

Royal Botanic Gardens

St Kilda Foreshore ⊙

St Kilda (p138)

Bohemian beachside suburb featuring a cast of characters from all walks of life, with a seedy history resisting gentrification.

⊙ Top Sights

St Kilda Foreshore

Explore
Melbourne

Centre Place (p31)
JOON WEI OOI/500PX ©

Explore

City Centre

Not just a business and shopping district, the city centre's wide main streets and laneways house many of Melbourne's top eateries and bars. Flanking the river, Federation Square is Melbourne's civic heart and home to several high-profile sights, while the constant buzz of retail radiates along Swanston and Elizabeth Sts towards the enormous Queen Victoria Market.

The Sights in a Day

☼ Start the day on chic Flinders Lane, treating yourself to one of the city's finest breakfasts at **Cumulus Inc** (p38) before wandering Melbourne's laneways. Check out the world-class street-art scene of stencils and graffiti along **Hosier Lane** (p34) and browse boutique shops such as **Craft Victoria** (p46).

☼ Grab authentic tapas from critically acclaimed **MoVida** (p40), before crossing the road to **Federation Square** (p24) – Melbourne's architecturally arresting centrepiece. Within its precinct, don't miss the **Ian Potter Centre: NGV Australia** (p34), home to Indigenous art and Australian modernist paintings. Leave time for **ACMI** (p25) and its multimedia exhibits, and a stroll through the adjoining parkland of **Birrarung Marr** (p26). Do a hook-turn and head back opposite Flinders Street Station to quench a well-earned thirst at **Young & Jackson** (p25), Melbourne's oldest pub.

☾ Dine on creative pan-Asian fare at **Supernormal** (p40) or line up for ridiculously good ramen at **Hakata Gensuke** (p38). Grab a preshow cocktail at **Bar Americano** (p42), before enjoying a night of high culture at the **Opera** (p45) or a rockin' evening at **Cherry** (p31) on ACDC Lane.

For a local's day in the City Centre, see p30.

◉ Top Sights

Federation Square (p24)

Birrarung Marr (p26)

Queen Victoria Market (p28)

◯ Local Life

Arcades & Laneways (p30)

♥ Best of Melbourne

Eating

Lee Ho Fook (p37)

Hakata Gensuke (p38)

Vue de Monde (p38)

Drinking & Nightlife

Madame Brussels (p42)

Rooftop Bar (p43)

Siglo (p42)

Getting There

🚃 **Train** The City Loop rings the central city, connecting Flinders St and Southern Cross stations with Flagstaff, Melbourne Central and Parliament stations.

🚋 **Tram** The city is crisscrossed with tracks; north–south trams head along Spencer, William, Elizabeth, Swanston and Spring Sts, and east–west trams ply Flinders, Collins, Bourke and La Trobe Sts. The whole of the city centre is a free tram zone.

Top Sights
Federation Square

While it's taken some time, Melburnians have finally come to embrace Federation Square, accepting it as the congregation place it was meant to be – somewhere to celebrate, protest, watch major sporting events or hang out on its deckchairs. Occupying a prominent city block, 'Fed Sq' is far from square: its undulating and patterned forecourt is paved with 460,000 hand-laid cobblestones from the Kimberley region, with sight lines to Melbourne's iconic landmarks, and its buildings are clad in a fractal-patterned reptilian skin.

👁 Map p32, E5

www.fedsquare.com

cnr Flinders & Swanston Sts

🚉 Flinders St

Ian Potter Centre: NGV Australia

Hidden away in the basement of Federation Square, the Ian Potter Centre: NGV Australia (p34) showcases an impressive collection of Australian works. Set over three levels, it's a mix of permanent (free) and temporary (ticketed) exhibitions, comprising paintings, decorative arts, photography, prints, sculpture and fashion. Highlights include the stunning Aboriginal permanent exhibition, colonial artist Tom Roberts' Shearing the Rams, modernist 'Angry Penguins' painters Sir Sidney Nolan and Albert Tucker, plus Fred Williams, John Brack and Howard Arkley.

Australian Centre for the Moving Image (ACMI)

Managing to educate, enthrall and entertain in equal parts, **ACMI** (☎03-8663 2200; www.acmi. net.au; Federation Sq; admission free; ⊙10am-5pm; ☒Flinders St) is a visual feast that pays homage to Australian cinema and TV. It offers insight into the modern-day Australian psyche, perhaps like no other museum can. Its floating screens don't discriminate against age, with TV shows, games and movies on-call for all. It's a great place to waste a day watching TV and not feel guilty about it

Federation Square Tours

Highly recommended (and free) tours depart from Monday to Saturday at 11am. Tours take in the intricacies of Federation Square's architecture and design, as well as some interesting Melbourne facts. Spots are limited, so arrive 10 minutes early.

☑ Top Tips

▶ Free tours of the Ian Potter Centre: NGV Australia are conducted daily at 11am, noon, 1pm and 2pm; free tours of ACMI are at 11am and 2.30pm daily.

▶ Grab one of the free deckchairs. Bring a hat and sunscreen; there's no shade outside.

▶ The square has free wi-fi, and mobile phone chargers are provided in the visitor centre.

✗ Take a Break

MoVida (p40) dishes up excellent tapas in street-art covered Hosier Lane.

Across the road, **Young & Jackson** (☎03-9650 3884; www.youngandjack sons.com.au; cnr Flinders & Swanston Sts; ⊙10am-late; ☎; ☒Flinders St) is a heritage pub that has been pouring beer since 1861. Head to the rooftop cider bar or stick to 1st-floor Chloe's Bar.

Top Sights
Birrarung Marr

The three-terraced Birrarung Marr is a welcome addition to Melbourne's patchwork of parks and gardens, featuring grassy knolls, river promenades, a thoughtful planting of indigenous flora and great viewpoints of the city and the river. There's also a scenic route to the Melbourne Cricket Ground (MCG) via the 'talking' William Barak Bridge – listen out for songs, words and sounds representing Melbourne's cultural diversity as you walk.

👁 Map p32, F5

Batman Ave

🚇 Flinders St

William Barak Bridge,

Federation Bells

The sculptural **Federation Bells** (www.federation bells.com.au; ⊙performances 8-9am, 12.30-1.30pm & 5-6pm; ⓇFlinders St) perch on the park's upper level and ring out daily like a robotic orchestra. There are 39 computer-controlled brass bells of various sizes and shapes, all with impressive acoustics, playing specially commissioned contemporary compositions.

Angel

Relocated from outside NGV International, the 10m-high, three-legged mosaic *Angel* is a vivid abstract sculpture by artist Deborah Halpern that resembles a dinosaur.

Speakers Corner

In the southeast corner of Birrarung Marr you'll find the original mounds used as soapboxes in the early 20th century. This was also used as a site for demonstrations, including when 50,000 people protested conscription during WWI. Near to here is a dried riverbed lined with ghost gums and palms, creating a tranquil billabong feel.

ArtPlay

Within an old railway building, **ArtPlay** (☑03-9664 7900; www.artplay.com.au; ⊙10am-4pm Wed-Sun; ⛲; ⓇFlinders St) hosts creative workshops for two- to 13-year-olds, getting them sewing, singing, painting and puppeteering, and has a cool playground out back.

William Barak Bridge

Stroll over the 'singing' William Barak Bridge (named after the Wurundjeri leader), which provides a scenic route to the MCG accompanied with sound installations. Listen out for songs, words and sounds representing Melbourne's cultural diversity as you walk.

☑ Top Tips

▶ Get online at www. federationbells.com.au to create your own composition to be played at the Federation Bells.

▶ Look out for photography ops, with each of the three terraces providing sightlines to the city's most famous landmarks.

▶ It's one of the best spots in the city to bring the kids, for both ArtPlay and its adventure playground.

✕ Take a Break

The bluestone bar **Riverland** (☑03-9662 1771; www. riverlandbar.com; vaults 1-9, Federation Wharf; ⊙8am-late; ⓇFlinders St) overlooking the Yarra River is an atmospheric spot to enjoy a drink or meal.

There are public barbecues along the banks of the Yarra, which are the perfect lunch spot for a sausage sizzle when the sun's out.

Top Sights
Queen Victoria Market

With over 600 traders, the Vic Market is the largest open-air market in the southern hemisphere. It's where Melburnians sniff out fresh produce among the booming cries of spruiking fishmongers and fruit-and-veg vendors. The deli hall is lined with everything from cheeses, wines and sausages to dips, truffle oil and kangaroo biltong.

Major restoration and redevelopment works are planned for the market, which are likely to run for several years. By late 2017 the fruit and vegetable traders should have moved into a striking new glass pavilion on Queen St.

◉ Map p32, D1

www.qvm.com.au

513 Elizabeth St

🕓 6am-2pm Tue & Thu, to 5pm Fri, to 3pm Sat, 9am-4pm Sun

🚇 Flagstaff

Produce

Saturday mornings are particularly buzzing, as market-goers breakfast to the sounds of buskers. Clothing and knick-knack stalls dominate on Sundays; they're big on variety, but don't come looking for style. (If you're after sheepskin moccasins or cheap T-shirts, you're in luck.)

Evening Markets

On Wednesday evenings from mid-November to the end of February the Summer Night Market takes over. It's a lively social event featuring hawker-style food stalls, bars and music and dance performances. There's also a Winter Night Market each Wednesday evening in August.

History

The market has been on this site for more than 130 years; before that, from 1837 to 1854, the old Melbourne Cemetery stood here. Remarkably, around 9000 bodies remain buried here, from underneath Shed F to the carpark leading to Franklin St. There's a small memorial on the corner of Queen and Therry Sts. Enquire online about Heritage & Cultural Tours.

☑ Top Tips

▶ Heritage, cultural and foodie tours run from the market; check online for details.

▶ Grab an Australiana souvenir such as Ugg boots or a Drizabone coat.

✕ Take a Break

The deli hall and fresh produce stalls have plenty of gourmet and organic goods for a picnic hamper. Choose from glistening olives, soft cheeses and local specialities of kangaroo biltong and regional Victorian wines. Head to nearby Flagstaff Gardens, or Botanic Gardens further afield, to enjoy.

Both **Padre Coffee** (www.padrecoffee.com. au; L Shed, String Bean Alley; ⏰7am-3pm Fri-Sun; ⛕Flagstaff) and Market Lane Coffee (p44) are excellent choices for grabbing an expertly-made coffee.

Local Life
Arcades & Laneways

Central Melbourne is a warren of 19th-century arcades and gritty-turned-hip cobbled bluestone laneways featuring fantastic street art, basement restaurants, boutiques and swanky bars. While the laneways are a celebration of edgy chic, the arcades are gleaming reminders of the grand sophistication that was 19th-century 'Marvelous Melbourne' during the city's gold-rush boom years.

❶ Campbell Arcade

Start underground at pink retro-tiled Campbell Arcade, also known as Degraves Subway. Built for the 1956 Olympics, it's home to a great collection of indie stores. **Sticky** (☎03-9654 8559; www.stickyinstitute.com; shop 10, Campbell Arcade, Flinders St Station; ⏰noon-6pm Mon-Sat; 🚆Flinders St) is a favourite haunt for those wanting to avoid mainstream press and pick up some hand-photocopied zines.

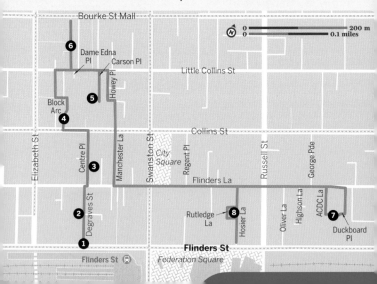

❷ Degraves St

Degraves St is a sophisticated laneway with boutiques and Parisian-style cafes, including **Degraves Espresso** (☑03-9654 1245; 23-25 Degraves St; ☺7am-10pm Mon-Sat, 8am-5pm Sun), a good spot for a coffee and to soak up the atmosphere.

❸ Centre Place

Centre Place is full of graffiti and cafes, and home to **Hell's Kitchen** (☑03-9654 5755; www.hellskitchenmelbourne.com; 1st fl, 20 Centre Pl; ☺noon-11pm Sun-Tue, to 1am Wed-Sat), the original hidden laneway bar. Head up a narrow flight of stairs to sip on classic cocktails and people-watch from the windows. It attracts a young, hip crowd and serves food.

❹ Block Arcade

Built in 1891, Block Arcade features etched-glass ceilings and sparkling mosaic floors that are based on Milan's Galleria Vittorio Emanuele plaza. Venture into **Gewürzhaus** (☑03-9639 6933; www.gewurzhaus.com.au; Block Arcade, 282 Collins St; ☺9.30am-6pm), a chef's dream stocking spices from around the world.

❺ Carson Place

From Little Collins St you'll pass Dame Edna Place, named after Moonee Ponds' favourite 'lady', before you reach Carson Place, another quintessential Melbourne lane. The **Butterfly Club** (☑03-9663 8107; www. thebutterflyclub.com; Carson Pl; ☺5pm-late Tue-Sun) here is an eccentric little cabaret with an extraordinary collection of kitsch; you're never quite sure what you're in for.

❻ Royal Arcade

This Parisian-style shopping **arcade** (www.royalarcade.com.au; 335 Bourke St Mall; ☒86, 96) was built between 1869 and 1870 and is Melbourne's oldest; the upper walls retain much of the original detail. The black-and-white chequered path leads to the mytho-logical figures of giant brothers Gog and Magog, perched atop the arched exit to Little Collins St. They've been striking the hour here since 1892.

❼ Rutledge & Hosier Lanes

Next stop is the street-art meccas of Hosier Lane and Rutledge Lane, where you can admire the colourful, clever graffiti. For the low-down on hidden pieces, sign up with **Melbourne Street Art Tours** (☑03-9328 5556; www. melbournestreettours.com; tours $69; ☺city centre 1.30pm Tue, Thu & Sat, Fitzroy 11am Sat) led by street-artist guides.

❽ AC/DC Lane & Duckboard Place

Finish down AC/DC Lane (named after the band, who are homegrown heroes) to **Cherry** (www.cherrybar.com.au; AC/DC Lane; ☺6pm-late Mon-Sat, 2pm-late Sun; ☒Flinders St), Melbourne's legendary rock 'n' roll bar where a welcoming, slightly anarchic spirit prevails. Live music and DJs play seven nights a week, and there's a long-standing soul night on Thursdays. From here, urban Duckboard Pl horseshoes around with more street art and hip restaurants.

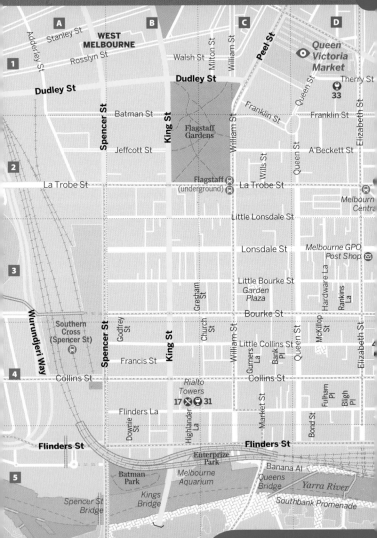

A **B** **C** **D**

Stanley St
Adderley St
WEST MELBOURNE
Rosslyn St
Walsh St
Milton St
William St
Peel St
Queen Victoria Market

1

Dudley St
Dudley St
Therry St
33

Batman St
King St
Flagstaff Gardens
William St
Franklin St
Queen St
Franklin St

2

Jeffcott St
A'Beckett St
Elizabeth St

Spencer St

La Trobe St
Flagstaff (underground)
La Trobe St
Wills St
Queen St

Little Lonsdale St

Melbourne Central

3

Lonsdale St
Melbourne GPO
Post Shop

Little Bourke St
Garden Plaza
Hardware La
Rankins La

Gresham St

Bourke St

Wurundjeri Way

Southern Cross (Spencer St)
Godfrey St
King St
Church St
William St
McKillop St
Queen St
Elizabeth St

4

Francis St
Little Collins St
Gurners La
Bank Pl

Spencer St

Collins St
Collins St
Fulham Pl
Bligh Pl

Rialto Towers
17 31

Flinders La
Downie St
Highlander La
Market St
Bond St

5

Flinders St
Flinders St

Spencer St Bridge
Batman Park
Kings Bridge
Enterprize Park
Melbourne Aquarium
Banana Al
Queens Bridge
Southbank Promenade
Yarra River

For reviews see

◉	Top Sights	p24
◉	Sights	p34
⊗	Eating	p37
◯	Drinking	p42
☆	Entertainment	p44
🛍	Shopping	p46

Sights

Hosier Lane
PUBLIC ART

1 ◉ Map p32, E4

Melbourne's most celebrated laneway for street art, Hosier Lane's cobbled length draws camera-wielding crowds snapping edgy graffiti, stencils and art installations. Subject matter runs to the mostly political and countercultural, spiced with irreverent humour; pieces change almost daily (not even a Banksy is safe here). Be sure to see Rutledge Lane (which horseshoes around Hosier), too. (🚇Flinders St)

Ian Potter Centre: NGV Australia
GALLERY

2 ◉ Map p32, F5

The National Gallery of Victoria's impressive Federation Square offshoot was set up to showcase its extraordinary collection of Australian works. Set over three levels, it's a mix of permanent (free) and temporary (ticketed) exhibitions, comprising paintings,

✓ Top Tip

Melbourne Street Tours

These three-hour walking **tours** (🕿03-9328 5556; www.melbournestreettours.com; tours $69; ⊙city centre 1.30pm Tue, Thu & Sat, Fitzroy 11am Sat) explore the street art of the city centre or Fitzroy. The guides are street artists themselves, so you'll get a good insight into this art form.

decorative arts, photography, prints, sculpture and fashion. Free tours are conducted daily at 11am, noon, 1pm and 2pm. (🕿03-8620 2222; www.ngv.vic.gov.au; Federation Sq; admission free; ⊙10am-5pm; 🚇Flinders St)

Chinatown
AREA

3 ◉ Map p32, F3

For more than 150 years this section of central Melbourne, now flanked by five traditional arches, has been the focal point for the city's Chinese community and it remains a vibrant neighbourhood of historic buildings filled with Chinese (and other Asian) restaurants. Come here for yum cha or to explore the attendant laneways for late-night dumplings or cocktails. Chinatown also hosts the city's Chinese New Year celebrations. (www.chinatownmelbourne.com.au; Little Bourke St, btwn Swanston & Exhibition Sts; 🚇Melbourne Central, Parliament)

Chinese Museum
MUSEUM

4 ◉ Map p32, F3

The fascinating history of Chinese people in Australia is showcased in this wonderful little museum. Start on level three, which features displays and artefacts relating to the gold-rush era and the xenophobic White Australia policy. Work your way down to the basement, where there are recreations of the hold of an immigrant boat, a temple and a typical house. Finish up in the Dragon Gallery on the ground floor. (🕿03-9662 2888; www.chinesemuseum.com.au; 22 Cohen Pl; adult/child $10/8.50; ⊙10am-4pm; 🚇Parliament)

Flinders Street Station

Flinders Street Station

HISTORIC BUILDING

5 Map p32, E5

If ever there were a true symbol of the city, Flinders Street Station would have to be it. Built in 1854, it was Melbourne's first railway station, and you'd be hard-pressed to find a Melburnian who hasn't uttered the phrase 'Meet me under the clocks' at some point (the popular rendezvous spot is located at the front entrance of the station). Stretching along the Yarra, it's a beautiful neoclassical building topped with a striking octagonal dome. (cnr Flinders & Swanston Sts; Flinders St)

Koorie Heritage Trust

CULTURAL CENTRE

6 Map p32, E5

Devoted to southeastern Aboriginal culture, this centre houses interesting artefacts and oral history. There's a shop and gallery downstairs while, upstairs, carefully preserved significant objects can be viewed in display cases and drawers. It also runs hour-long tours along the Yarra during summer, evoking the history and memories that lie beneath the modern city (book online). (03-8662 6300; www.koorie heritagetrust.com; Yarra Building, Federation Sq; tours adult/child $33/17; 10am-5pm; Flinders St)

Old Melbourne Gaol

HISTORIC BUILDING

7 ⊙ Map p32, F2

Built in 1841, this forbidding bluestone prison was in operation until 1929. It's now one of Melbourne's most popular museums, where you can tour the tiny, bleak cells. Around 135 people were hanged here, including Ned Kelly, Australia's most infamous bushranger, in 1880; one of his death masks is on display. Visits include the Police Watch House Experience, where you get 'arrested' and thrown in the slammer (more fun than it sounds). (☏03-8663 7228; www.oldmelbournegaol.com.au; 337 Russell St; adult/child/family $25/14/55; ☉9.30am-5pm; 🚇Melbourne Central)

State Library of Victoria

LIBRARY

8 ⊙ Map p32, E2

This grand neoclassical building has been at the forefront of Melbourne's literary scene since it opened in 1856. When its epicentre, the gorgeous octagonal La Trobe Reading Room,

Top Tip

City Circle Tram

Designed primarily for tourists, this **free tram service** (☏13 16 38; www. ptv.vic.gov.au; ☉10am-6pm Sun-Wed, to 9pm Thu-Sat; 🚋35) travels around the city centre, passing many city sights along the way. It runs every 12 minutes or so and there's a recorded commentary.

was completed in 1913, its reinforced-concrete dome was the largest of its kind in the world; its natural light illuminates the ornate plasterwork and the studious Melbourne writers who come here to pen their works. For visitors, the highlight is the fascinating collection showcased in the Dome Galleries. (☏03-8664 7002; www.slv.vic.gov.au; 328 Swanston St; ☉10am-9pm Mon-Thu, to 6pm Fri-Sun, galleries 10am-5pm; 🚇Melbourne Central)

Old Treasury Building

MUSEUM

9 ⊙ Map p32, G4

The fine neoclassical architecture of the Old Treasury (1862), designed by JJ Clarke, is a telling mix of hubris and functionality. The basement vaults were built to house the millions of pounds' worth of loot that came from the Victorian goldfields and now feature multimedia displays telling stories from that era. Also downstairs is the 1920s caretaker's flat and a reproduction of the 70kg *Welcome Stranger* nugget, found in 1869. (☏03-9651 2233; www.oldtreasurybuilding.org.au; 20 Spring St; admission free; ☉10am-4pm Sun-Fri; 🚇Parliament)

Parliament House

HISTORIC BUILDING

10 ⊙ Map p32, G3

The grand steps of Victoria's parliament (1856) are often dotted with slow-moving, tulle-wearing brides smiling for the camera, or placard-holding protesters doing the same. On sitting days the public is welcome to view proceedings from the galleries. On

Understand
Street Art

Melbourne's urban landscape is a beacon for visitors from all around the world. Dozens of laneway walls provide an outdoor canvas for paste-up, mural and stencil art. Local street artists of note include ghostpatrol, miso, Tai Snaith and Ha-Ha (the latter for his iconic Ned Kelly images – move aside, Sidney Nolan).

Melbourne's scene was helped by the legacy of renowned international street artists such as Keith Haring (1958–1990), the New York graffiti artist who visited in 1984. He was commissioned to paint large-scale murals at NGV International and what was then the Collingwood Technical School on Johnston St; the latter work still exists today (visible next door to the Tote music club).

The city's street-art scene received further recognition through Banksy, who stencilled extensively during a visit in 2003. While several of his works remain, many have disappeared (some accidentally painted over by unsuspecting workers). Some great spots to check out the city's street art include Hosier and Rutledge Lane, Caledonian Lane, Blender Lane and Union Lane.

nonsitting days, there are eight guided tours a day; times are posted online and on a sign by the door. Numbers are limited, so aim to arrive at least 15 minutes before time. (☏03-9651 8568; www.parliament.vic.gov.au; Spring St; admission free; ⏰8.30am-5.30pm Mon-Fri; ⓇParliament)

Eating

Lee Ho Fook CHINESE $$$

11 ✕ Map p32, F5

Occupying an old brick warehouse down a fabulously skungy laneway, Lee Ho Fook is the epitome of modern Chinese culinary wizardry. The kitchen packs an extraordinary amount of flavour into signature dishes such as crispy eggplant with red vinegar, chicken crackling, liquorice wagyu

beef, and crab and scallop rice with homemade XO sauce. The service is terrific too. (☏03-9077 6261; www.leehofook.com.au; 11-15 Duckboard Pl; mains $32-42; ⏰noon-2.30pm & 6-11pm Mon-Fri, 6-11pm Sat & Sun; ⓇParliament)

Chin Chin SOUTHEAST ASIAN $$

12 ✕ Map p32, F4

Insanely popular, and for good reason, chic Chin Chin serves delicious Southeast Asian hawker-style food designed as shared plates. It's housed in a glammed-up old warehouse with a real New York feel, and while there are no bookings, you can fill in time at the Go Go Bar downstairs until there's space. (☏03-8663 2000; www.chinchinrestaurant.com.au; 125 Flinders Lane; mains $20-39; ⏰11am-late; ⓇFlinders St)

Supernormal

ASIAN $$

13 Map p32, E4

Drawing on his years spent in Shanghai and Hong Kong, chef Andrew McConnell presents a creative selection of pan-Asian sharing dishes, from dumplings to raw seafood to slow-cooked Sichuan lamb. Even if you don't dine in, stop by for his now-famous takeaway New England lobster roll. No dinner bookings, so get here early to put your name on the list. (☑03-9650 8688; www.supernormal.net.au; 180 Flinders Lane; dishes $16-39; ⏰11am-11pm; 🚆Flinders St)

Hakata Gensuke

RAMEN $

14 Map p32, F3

Gensuke is one of those places that only does one thing and does it extraordinarily well. In this case it's *tonkotsu* (pork broth) ramen. Choose from three types (signature, sesame-infused 'black' or spicy 'god fire') and then order extra toppings (marinated *cha-shu* pork, egg, seaweed, black fungus). Inevitably there will be a queue, but it's well worth the wait.

☑️ Top Tip

No Reservations

Many of the city's best restaurants have a 'no bookings' policy, so clued-up locals arrive early. Most places will take your number and call you when a table becomes free, so you don't have to hang around.

(☑03-9663 6342; www.gensuke.com.au; 168 Russell St; mains $13-14; ⏰11.30am-2.45pm & 5-9.30pm Mon-Fri, noon-9.30pm Sat & Sun; 🚆Parliament)

Cumulus Inc

MODERN AUSTRALIAN $$$

15 Map p32, G4

This bustling informal eatery focuses on beautiful produce and simple but artful cooking, served at the long marble bar and at little round tables dotted about. Dinner reservations are only taken for groups, so expect to queue. Upstairs is the Cumulus Up wine bar. (☑03-9650 1445; www.cumulusinc.com.au; 45 Flinders Lane; breakfast $14-18, mains $36-44; ⏰7am-11pm; 🚆Parliament)

Coda

SOUTHEAST ASIAN $$$

16 Map p32, F4

Coda has a wonderful basement ambience, with exposed light bulbs and roughly stripped walls. Its innovative menu leans heavily towards Southeast Asian flavours, but Japanese, Korean, French and Italian influences are all apparent. While there are larger dishes made for sharing, the single-serve bites are particularly good. (☑03-9650 3155; www.codarestaurant.com.au; basement, 141 Flinders Lane; larger plates $39-46; ⏰noon-3pm & 6pm-late; 🚆Flinders St)

Vue de Monde

MODERN AUSTRALIAN $$$

17 Map p32, B4

Surveying the world from the old observation deck of the Rialto tower, Melbourne's favoured spot for occasion

GREG ELMS/GETTY IMAGES ©

Dining at Longrain

dining has views to match its storied reputation. Visionary chef Shannon Bennett produces sophisticated set menus showcasing the very best Australian ingredients. Book well – months – ahead. (☏03-9691 3888; www.vuedemonde.com.au; 55th fl, Rialto, 525 Collins St; set menu $230-275; ☉6-11pm Mon-Wed, noon-2pm & 6-11pm Thu-Sun; ☐Southern Cross)

Grossi Florentino ITALIAN $$$

18 ✗ Map p32, F3

Over-the-top gilded plasterwork, chandeliers and 1930s Florentine Renaissance murals engender a real sense of occasion at this top-notch Italian restaurant. Decadent set menus are accompanied by exquisite canapés and delicious bread, and the service is extremely slick. The Grill and Cellar Bar below offer more affordable options. (☏03-9662 1811; www.grossiflorentino.com; 1st fl, 80 Bourke St; 2-course lunch $65, 3-course dinner $140; ☉noon-2.30pm & 6pm-late Mon-Fri, 6pm-late Sat; ☐Parliament)

Longrain THAI $$$

19 ✗ Map p32, G3

Get in early or expect a long wait (sip a drink and relax, they suggest) before sampling Longrain's innovative Thai cuisine. The communal tables don't exactly work for a romantic date, but they're great for checking out everyone

Local Life
Pellegrini's

The Italian equivalent of a classic 1950s diner, locally famous **Pellegrini's** (☎03-9662 1885; 66 Bourke St; mains $18; ☉8am-11pm Mon-Sat, noon-8pm Sun; ☒Parliament) has remained genuinely unchanged for decades. There's no menu with prices; the staff will tell you what's available. Expect classic Italian comfort food: lasagne, spaghetti bolognese and big slabs of cake. Service can be brusque, but that's all part of the experience.

else's meals. Dishes are designed to be shared; try the pork-and-prawn eggnet. (☎03-9671 3151; www.longrain.com; 44 Little Bourke St; mains $30-40; ☉6-10pm Mon-Thu, noon-3pm & 5.30pm-late Fri, 5.30pm-late Sat & Sun; ☒Parliament)

Tonka   INDIAN $$$

Tonka's dining room (see 11 ☒ Map p32, F5) is long, elegant and very white, with billowy white mesh forming clouds overhead. The food, however, is gloriously technicolour. The punchy flavours of Indian cuisine are combined with unexpected elements – burrata, for instance, served with coriander relish and charred roti. Get the clued-up sommelier to recommend appropriate matches from the extraordinary wine list. (☎03-9650 3155; www.tonkarestaurant.com.au; 20 Duckboard Pl; mains $26-40; ☉noon-3pm & 6pm-late Mon-Sat; ☒Parliament)

Mamasita   MEXICAN $$

20 ☒ Map p32, G4

The restaurant responsible for kicking off Melbourne's obsession with authentic Mexican street food, Mamasita is still one of the very best. The char-grilled corn sprinkled with cheese and chipotle mayo is legendary, and there's a fantastic range of tacos and a mammoth selection of tequila. It doesn't take reservations for dinner, so prepare to wait. (☎03-9650 3821; www.mamasita.com.au; 1st fl, 11 Collins St; tacos $7, quesadillas $15, shared plates $24-27; ☉5-11pm Sun-Wed, noon-midnight Thu-Sat; ☒Parliament)

MoVida   TAPAS $$

21 ☒ Map p32, E5

MoVida's location in much-graffitied Hosier Lane is about as Melbourne as it gets. Line up by the bar, cluster around little window tables or, if you've booked, take a seat in the dining area for fantastic Spanish tapas and *raciones*. MoVida Next Door – yes, right next door – is the perfect place for preshow beers and tapas. (☎03-9663 3038; www.movida.com.au; 1 Hosier Lane; tapas $4-8, raciones $16-34; ☉noon-late; ☒Flinders St)

Flower Drum   CHINESE $$

22 ☒ Map p32, F3

Established in 1975, Flower Drum continues to be Melbourne's most celebrated Chinese restaurant, imparting a charmingly old-fashioned ambience. The sumptuous but simple Cantonese food (from a menu that changes daily) is delivered with the top-notch service

Understand

Indigenous Melbourne

The earliest records of Australia's Indigenous people inhabiting the land date back around 52,000 years. At the time they hunted the giant marsupials that then roamed Victoria and Australia, among them a species of wombat the size of a rhinoceros and possibly even a giant, metre-long platypus. The oral history of Indigenous Australians has its own version of Victoria's prehistory. For the Wurundjeri people, who lived in the catchment of the Yarra River where Melbourne is today, the land and the people were created in the Dreaming by the spirit Bunjil – 'the great one, old head-man, eagle hawk' – who continues to watch over all from Tharangalk-bek, the home of the spirits in the sky.

The area around Melbourne has been inhabited for over 40,000 years by Indigenous people. The Yarra River and its tributaries were the lands of the Woiwurrung, one of five groups that make up the Kulin nation, which inhabited the central slice of what is now Victoria. In Kulin spirituality, the land and the people were created in the Dreaming by the spirit Bunjil, the great eagle (several prominent statues of Bunjil adorn Melbourne today).

A complex system of customs and laws governed everyday life, and the custodianship of the land devolved to smaller tribal groupings. The Woiwurrung community that lived in what is now Melbourne were known as the Wurundjeri. They traded and often celebrated with their coastal counterparts, the Boonwurrung, among the towering red gums, tea trees and ferns of the river's edge, as well as with other Kulin clans from the north and west.

As the flood-prone rivers and creeks broke their banks in winter, bark shelters were built north in the ranges. Possums were hunted for their meat and skinned to make cloaks. During summer, camps were made along the Yarra and Maribyrnong Rivers and Merri Creek. Food – game, grubs, seafood, native greens and roots – was plentiful. Wurundjeri men and women were compelled to marry outside the tribe, requiring complex forms of diplomacy. Ceremonies and bouts of ritual combat were frequent.

Some of the best places in Melbourne to gain an insight into Indigenous Australian culture include the Bunjilaka Aboriginal Culture Centre at the Melbourne Museum (p122), Birrarung Marr (p26), Koorie Heritage Trust (p35) and on the Aboriginal Heritage Walk in the Royal Botanic Gardens (75).

you'd expect in such elegant surroundings. (📞03-9662 3655; www.flowerdrum. melbourne; 1st fl, 17 Market Lane; mains $18-40; ⏱noon-3pm & 6-11pm Mon-Sat, 6-10.30pm Sun; 🛜; 🚉Parliament)

HuTong Dumpling Bar   CHINESE $$

23 🍴 Map p32, F3

HuTong's reputation for divine *xiao long bao* means getting a lunchtime seat anywhere in this three-level building isn't easy. Downstairs, watch chefs make the delicate dumplings, then hope they don't watch you making a mess eating them. (📞03-9650 8128; www.hutong.com.au; 14-16 Market Lane; mains $14-31; ⏱11.30am-3pm & 5.30-10.30pm; 🚉Parliament)

Drinking

Bar Americano   COCKTAIL BAR

24 🍺 Map p32, E4

A hideaway bar in a lane off Howey Pl, Bar Americano is a teensy standing-room-only affair with black-and-white chequered floors and a subtle air of speakeasy. Once it hits its 14-person max, the grille gets pulled shut. The cocktails here don't come cheap, but they do come superb. (www.baramericano.com.au; 20 Presgrave Pl; ⏱5pm-1am Mon-Sat; 🚉Flinders St)

Heartbreaker   BAR

25 🍺 Map p32, F2

Black walls, red lights, random taxidermy, craft beer, a big selection of bourbon, and rock and punk on the sound system – all the prerequisites, in fact, for a hard-rocking good time. (📞03-9041 0856; www.heartbreakerbar.com. au; 234a Russell St; ⏱5pm-3am Mon-Sat, to 11pm Sun; 🚉Melbourne Central)

Madame Brussels   ROOFTOP BAR

26 🍺 Map p32, G3

Head up to this wonderful rooftop terrace if you've had it with Melbourne-moody and all that dark wood. Although it's named for a famous 19th-century brothel owner, it feels like a camp 1960s country club, with staff dressed for a spot of tennis. (📞03-9662 2775; www.madamebrussels. com; 3rd fl, 57-59 Bourke St; ⏱noon-11pm Sun-Wed, to 1am Thu-Sat; 🚉Parliament)

Siglo   ROOFTOP BAR

27 🍺 Map p32, G3

Siglo's sought-after terrace comes with Parisian flair, wafting cigar smoke and serious drinks. Mull over a classic cocktail, snack on upper-crust morsels and admire the 19th-century vista over Parliament and St Patrick's Cathedral. Entry is via the **Supper Club** (1st fl, 161 Spring St; 🚉Parliament), which is similarly unsigned. (📞03-9654 6631; www.siglobar.com.au; 2nd fl, 161 Spring St; ⏱5pm-3am)

Croft Institute   BAR

28 🍺 Map p32, F3

Hidden in a graffitied laneway off a laneway, the slightly creepy Croft is a laboratory-themed bar downstairs, while upstairs at weekends the 1950s-

Pellegrini's (p40)

themed gymnasium opens as a club. There's a $5 cover charge for Friday and Saturday nights. (www.thecroftinstitute.com. au; 21 Croft Alley; ⏲5pm-midnight Mon-Thu, 5pm-3am Fri, 8pm-3am Sat; ⛁86, 96)

Cookie BAR

29 Map p32, E3

Part bar, part Thai restaurant, this kooky-cool venue with grand bones is one of the more enduring rites of passage of the Melbourne night. The bar is unbelievably well stocked with fine whiskies, wines, and plenty of craft beers among the more than 200 brews on offer. (☏03-9663 7660; www.cookie. net.au; 1st fl, Curtin House, 252 Swanston St; ⏲noon-3am; ⛢Melbourne Central)

Boilermaker House BAR

30 Map p32, E3

A real surprise on busy, workaday Lonsdale St, this dimly lit haven of urbanity has a phenomenal 850 whiskies on its list, along with 12 craft beers on tap and a further 40 by the bottle. (www. boilermakerhouse.com.au; 209-211 Lonsdale St; ⏲4pm-3am; ⛢Melbourne Central)

Rooftop Bar ROOFTOP BAR

This bar sits at dizzying heights atop happening Curtin House (see **29** Map p32, E3). In summer it transforms into an outdoor cinema with striped deckchairs and a calendar of new and classic favourite flicks. (☏03-9654 5394; www.rooftopcinema.com.au; 6th fl,

Curtin House, 252 Swanston St; ☉noon-1am; 🚊Melbourne Central)

Lui Bar

COCKTAIL BAR

31 🚇 Map p32, B4

Some people are happy to shell out $36 for the view from the 120m-high Melbourne Star, but we'd much rather spend $25 on a cocktail at this so-phisticated bar perched 236m up the Rialto tower. Best get there early (and nicely dressed) to claim your table. (☎03-9691 3888; www.vuedemonde.com.au; 55th fl, Rialto, 525 Collins St; ☉5.30pm-midnight Mon-Wed, 11.30am-1am Thu, 11.30am-3am Fri & Sat, 11.30am-midnight Sun; 🚊Southern Cross)

Garden State Hotel

BAR

32 🚇 Map p32, F4

Just as in a grand English garden, there are orderly bits, wild bits and little dark nooks in this so-hot-right-now multipurpose venue. The best part is the chandelier-festooned Rose Garden cocktail bar in the basement. (☎03-8396 5777; www.gardenstatehotel.com.au; 101 Flinders Lane; ☉11am-late; 🛜; 🚊Flinders St)

Market Lane Coffee

CAFE

33 🚇 Map p32, D1

It's all about the super-strong coffee at this branch of Market Lane. It serves a few pastries, too, but as it's right opposite Queen Victoria Market there's no shortage of snacks at hand to enjoy with your takeaway cup. There's another branch in the market's deli hall. (www.marketlane.com.au; 109-111 Therry St; ☉7am-4pm; 🚊Melbourne Central)

Arbory

BAR

34 🚇 Map p32, E5

Situated close to the Yarra, Arbory occupies the decommissioned platform for the Sandridge train line at the edge of Flinders Street Station. Come for the view of the Arts Centre across the water, stay for the espresso martinis. The food's not bad either. (☎03-8648 7644; www.arbory.com.au; 1 Flinders Walk; ☉7.30am-late; 🚊Flinders St)

Entertainment

Forum

CONCERT VENUE

35 ⭐ Map p32, F5

One of the city's most atmospheric live-music venues, the Forum's strik-ing over-the-top exterior houses an equally interesting interior, with the southern night sky rendered on the domed ceiling. (☎1300 111 011; www.forummelbourne.com.au; 150-152 Flinders St; 🚊Flinders St)

Her Majesty's Theatre

THEATRE

36 ⭐ Map p32, F3

On the outside Her Maj is painted-brick Second Empire; on the inside it's 1930s Moderne. It's been the home of musical comedy since 1880 and it's still going strong. (☎03-8643 3300; www.hmt.com.au; 219 Exhibition St; 🚊Parliament)

ALEKSANDAR TODOROVIC/SHUTTERSTOCK ©

Forum

Wheeler Centre ARTS CENTRE

37 ⭐ Map p32, E2

Set up by Lonely Planet founders Maureen and Tony Wheeler to show-case 'books, writing and ideas', this centre has become an important part of the city's intellectual life, hosting regular talks by distinguished speakers on a vast range of subjects. (📞03-9094 7800; www.wheelercentre.com; 176 Little Lonsdale St; Ⓡ Melbourne Central)

Bennetts Lane JAZZ

38 ⭐ Map p32, F2

Bennetts Lane has long been the boiler room of Melbourne jazz.

It attracts the cream of local and international talent and an audience that knows when it's time to applaud a solo. Beyond the cosy front bar is another space reserved for big gigs. (📞03-9663 2856; www.bennettslane.com; 25 Bennetts Lane; Ⓡ Melbourne Central)

Melbourne Opera OPERA

39 ⭐ Map p32, E4

A not-for-profit company that performs classic and light opera in various venues, including the **Regent Theatre** (📞1300 111 011; www.marrinerthe atres.com.au; 191 Collins St; Ⓡ Flinders St). (📞03-9614 4188; www.melbourneopera.com)

Shopping

Craft Victoria
ARTS & CRAFTS

40 🔒 Map p32, G4

This retail arm of Craft Victoria showcases handmade goods, mainly by Victorian artists and artisans. Its range of jewellery, textiles, accessories, glass and ceramics makes for some wonderful mementos of Melbourne. There are also a few galleries with changing exhibitions; admission is free. (☑03-9650 7775; www.craft.org.au; 31 Flinders Lane; ◷11am-6pm Mon-Sat; ☒Parliament)

Top Tip
Tickets

Tickets for concerts, theatre, comedy, sports and other events are usually available from one of the following agencies:

Halftix (www.halftixmelbourne.com; Melbourne Town Hall, 90-120 Swanston St; ◷10am-2pm Mon, 11am-6pm Tue-Fri, 10am-4pm Sat; ☒Flinders St) Discounted theatre tickets are sold on the day of performance.

Moshtix (www.moshtix.com.au)

Ticketek (www.ticketek.com.au; 252 Exhibition St; ◷9am-5pm Mon-Fri, 10am-3pm Sat)

Ticketmaster (☑1300 111 011; www.ticketmaster.com.au; Forum, 150-152 Flinders St; ◷9am-6pm Mon-Fri)

Alpha60
FASHION & ACCESSORIES

41 🔒 Map p32, E4

Melbourne has a reputation for top-notch retail spaces, but this place is just showing off. Alpha60's signature store is hidden within the chapter house of St Paul's Cathedral, where women's clothing is displayed on a phalanx of mannequins while giant projections of roosters keep watch. (☑03-9663 3002; www.alpha60.com.au; 2nd fl, 209 Flinders Lane; ◷10am-6pm; ☒Flinders St)

Basement Discs
MUSIC

42 🔒 Map p32, D4

Apart from a range of CD titles across all genres, Basement Discs has regular in-store performances by big-name touring and local acts. (☑03-9654 1110; www.basementdiscs.com.au; 24 Block Pl; ◷10am-6pm; ☒Flinders St)

Hill of Content
BOOKS

43 🔒 Map p32, F3

Melbourne's oldest bookshop (established 1922) has a range of general titles and an extensive stock of books on art, classics and poetry. (☑03-9662 9472; www.hillofcontentbookshop.com; 86 Bourke St; ◷10am-6pm Sat-Thu, to 8pm Fri; ☒Parliament)

Melbournalia
GIFTS & SOUVENIRS

44 🔒 Map p32, G3

Stock up on interesting souvenirs by more than 100 local designers. (☑03-9663 3751; www.melbournalia.com.au; 50 Bourke St; ◷10am-7pm; ☒Parliament)

LEON MORRIS/GETTY IMAGES ©

Live jazz at Bennetts Lane (p45)

Original & Authentic Aboriginal Art
ART

For over 20 years this centrally located gallery (see **43** 🔒 Map p32, F3) has sourced Indigenous art from across the country. It subscribes to the City of Melbourne's code of practice for Indigenous art, ensuring authenticity and ethical dealings with artists. (📞03-9663 5133; www.originalandauthenticaboriginalart.com; 90 Bourke St; ⏰10am-6pm; 🚆Parliament)

City Hatters
HATS

45 🔒 Map p32, E5

Located beside the main entrance to Flinders Street Station, this evoca-

tively old-fashioned store is the most convenient place to purchase an iconic Akubra hat, a kangaroo-leather sun hat or something a little more unique. (📞03-9614 3294; www.cityhatters.com.au; 211 Flinders St; ⏰9am-5pm; 🚆Flinders St)

RM Williams
CLOTHING

46 🔒 Map p32, E2

An Aussie icon, even for city slickers, this brand will kit you out in stylish essentials for working the land, including a pair of its famous boots. (📞03-9663 7126; www.rmwilliams.com; Melbourne Central, cnr La Trobe & Swanston Sts; ⏰10am-7pm Sat-Wed, to 9pm Thu & Fri; 🚆Melbourne Central)

Explore

Southbank & Docklands

It's hard to imagine that, before the 1980s, Southbank was a gritty industrial zone supporting a major port. Now its pleasant riverside promenade is crammed with restaurants and hotels, while the presence of some of the city's top arts institutions makes it an essential visit. To the city's west, the once working wharves of Docklands have given birth to a mini city of apartments, offices, restaurants and parks.

The Sights in a Day

☀ Get your bearings atop the **Melbourne Star** (p54) observation wheel, looking over the city and beyond. Once back on ground, browse the Dockland's precinct of restaurants, before jumping on the free City Circle Tram to scuttle over the river to another emerging waterfront development along South Wharf. Grab lunch at one of many new places along the river, either **Bangpop** (p54) for Thai or **Boatbuilders Yard** (p56) for barbecue and beer.

☀ Stroll along the river en route to picturesque Southbank. Enjoy dazzling city views, best taken from atop **Eureka Skydeck** (p53). Make your way up St Kilda Rd to see masterpieces by Picasso and the Impressionists at **NGV International** (p50). Afterwards, drop into the box office at **Arts Centre Melbourne** (p53) to see what shows take your fancy.

☽ At sunset head back along the Yarra for a drink at **Ponyfish Island** (p56). After drinking up an appetite, make your way to **Crown** (p53) for its upmarket restaurants such as **Spice Temple** (p54), which you're advised to book in advance. In the evening, catch a show at the Arts Centre, enjoy a night at the casino, or wander the promenade and watch street performers along Southbank.

◉ Top Sights

NGV International (p50)

♥ Best of Melbourne

Museums & Galleries

NGV International (p50)

ACCA (p53)

Entertainment

Melbourne Theatre Company (p56)

Chunky Move (p58)

Melbourne Recital Centre (p57)

Arts Centre Melbourne (p53)

Getting There

🚆 **Train** Southern Cross is one of Melbourne's two major train stations and the terminus for regional and interstate trains. Flinders Street Station is connected to Southbank by three bridges.

🚊 **Tram** Various routes run along St Kilda Rd from the city, stopping outside the Arts Centre. Tram 55 stops east of the Crown complex.

Top Sights
NGV International

Housed in a vast, brutally beautiful, bunker-like building, the international branch of the National Gallery of Victoria has an expansive collection that runs the gamut from the ancient to the bleeding edge. Key works include a Rembrandt self-portrait, Tiepolo's *The Banquet of Cleopatra* and Turner's otherworldly *Falls of Schaffhausen*. It's also home to Picasso's *Weeping Woman*, which was the victim of an art heist in 1986. Regular blockbuster exhibitions (prices vary) draw the crowds.

Map p52, E3

03-8662 1555

www.ngv.vic.gov.au

180 St Kilda Rd, Southbank

admission free

10am-5pm

Flinders St

Paintings

Key works include a Rembrandt, a Tiepolo and a Bonnard. You might also bump into a Monet, a Modigliani, a Bacon or a Turner. NGV is home to Picasso's *Weeping Woman,* which was the victim of an art heist in 1986. It's also home to *Head of a Man,* which remains an international source of conjecture over its authenticity.

Asian Art

The gallery boasts an excellent Asian decorative arts collection, with beautiful pieces on display including Tibetan mandalas, Burmese lacquered betel boxes, Chinese porcelain, Japanese pottery and sculptures of Hindu deities.

Antiquities

Artifacts and relics from Ancient Egypt and Greece are on display, as well as Middle Eastern and European items. Central America is also well represented in its Art of Mesoamerica collection comprising 12th-century masks, jewellery and vessels.

Art & Design

NGV has a fantastic modern art and design collection, spanning paintings, sculptures, photography, fashion, textiles and multimedia from the Americas and Europe.

Architecture

Designed by architect Roy Grounds, the NGV building was controversial when it was completed in 1967 but has come to be respected as a modernist masterpiece. Make sure you wander through the foyer to the Great Hall, with its extraordinary stained-glass ceiling, and continue out onto the sculpture lawn.

☑ Top Tips

▶ Free 45-minute tours run hourly from 11am to 2pm, and hour-long tours at midday and 2pm, focusing on different parts of the collection.

▶ Most paintings come with detailed captions, so an audioguide isn't essential.

▶ Australian artwork is shown at the Ian Potter Centre: NGV Australia (p34) at nearby Federation Square.

▶ The museum has free wi-fi.

✗ Take a Break

Take a short stroll to Southbank's riverfront promenade and grab a drink and light snack at the fantastic hidden nook, Ponyfish Island. (p56)

There are a few on-site dining options including the Garden Restaurant, a tea room and a cafe.

For reviews see	
◆ Top Sights	p50
◎ Sights	p53
⊗ Eating	p54
❏ Drinking	p56
☆ Entertainment	p56
⊜ Shopping	p58

Sights

Kayak Melbourne
KAYAKING

1 ◎ Map p52, E2

Ninety-minute City Sights tours paddle past Southbank to Docklands, while two-hour River to Sky tours include entry to the Eureka Skydeck (p53). You can also start your day saluting the sun on a two-hour Yoga Sunrise tour, or end it with a 2½-hour Moonlight tour starting from Docklands. (☏0418 106 427; www.kayakmelbourne.com.au; Alexandra Gardens, Boathouse Dr, Southbank; tours $82-110; ☐11, 48)

Arts Centre Melbourne
ARTS CENTRE

2 ◎ Map p52, E3

The Arts Centre is made up of two separate buildings, Hamer Hall and the Theatres Building (under the spire, including a free gallery space with changing exhibitions), linked by a series of landscaped walkways. Tours of the theatres and exhibitions leave daily at 11am (adult/child $20/15); the Sunday tour includes the backstage areas. (☏1300 182 183; www.artscentremelbourne.com.au; 100 St Kilda Rd, Southbank; ☺box office 9am-8.30pm Mon-Fri, 10am-5pm Sat; ☐Flinders St)

Australian Centre for Contemporary Art
GALLERY

3 ◎ Map p52, E4

ACCA is one of Australia's most exciting and challenging contemporary galleries, showcasing the work of a range of local and international artists. The building is, fittingly, sculptural, with a rusted exterior evoking the factories that once stood on the site, and a soaring interior designed to house often massive installations. (ACCA; ☏03-9697 9999; www.accaonline.org.au; 111 Sturt St, Southbank; admission free; ☺10am-5pm Tue-Sun; ☐1)

Eureka Skydeck
VIEWPOINT

4 ◎ Map p52, E3

Melbourne's tallest building, the 297m-high Eureka Tower was built in 2006, and a wild elevator ride takes you to its 88 floors in less than 40 seconds (check out the photo on the elevator floor if there's time). The Edge – a slightly sadistic glass cube – cantilevers you out of the building; you've got no choice but to look down. (☏03-9693 8888; www.eurekaskydeck.com.au; 7 Riverside Quay, Southbank; adult/child $20/12, Edge extra $12/8; ☺10am-10pm; ☐Flinders St)

Crown
CASINO

5 ◎ Map p52, D3

The Crown complex sprawls across two city blocks and includes three luxury hotels, top restaurants and a casino that's open 24/7. It's another world with its no-natural-light interior, in which the hours fly by. Thrown in for good measure are waterfalls, fireballs, cinemas and a variety of nightclubs. The complex is also home to luxury retailers, chain stores and speciality shops, as well as bars, cafes and a food hall. (☑03-9292 8888; www.crownmelbourne.com.au; 8 Whiteman St, Southbank; 🚋12, 55, 96, 109)

Melbourne Star VIEWPOINT

6 ⊙ Map p52, A1

Joining the London Eye and Singapore Flyer, this giant observation wheel has glass cabins that take you up 120m for 360-degree views of the city, Port Phillip Bay and even further afield to Geelong and the Dandenongs. Rides last 30 minutes. For an extra $10 you can head back for another ride at night to see the bright lights of the city. (☑03-8688 9688; www.melbournestar.com; 101 Waterfront Way, Docklands; adult/child $36/22; ⊙11am-7.30pm Sun-Thu, to 9pm Fri & Sat May–mid-Sep, to 10pm mid-Sep–Apr; 🚋35, 70, 86)

Eating

Spice Temple CHINESE $$$

7 🍴 Map p52, D3

When he's not at Rockpool (p54) next door or in one of his Sydney restaurants, well-known chef Neil Perry pays homage to the spicy cuisines of China's central provinces at this excellent waterfront eatery. By day you can gaze at the river while you tuck into the $49 yum cha banquet. By night, descend to the atmospheric darkened tabernacle beneath. (☑03-8679 1888; www.rockpool.com; Crown, Yarra Promenade, Southbank; mains $15-52; ⊙6-11pm Mon-Wed, noon-3pm & 6-11pm Thu-Sun; 🍸; 🚋55)

Rockpool Bar & Grill STEAK $$$

8 🍴 Map p52, D3

The Melbourne outpost of Neil Perry's empire offers his signature seafood raw bar, but the star is the dry-aged beef. The masculine space is simple and stylish, as is the menu. The bar offers the same menu and service with the bonus of an additional, cheaper menu ($24 to $29). (☑03-8648 1900; www.rockpool.com; Crown, Yarra Promenade, Southbank; mains $35-70; ⊙noon-2.30pm & 6-11pm Sun-Fri, 6-11pm Sat; 🚋55)

Bangpop THAI $$

9 🍴 Map p52, C3

Bangpop breathes a bit of colour and vibrancy into the area with its bar made from Lego and dangling filament bulbs. Flavour-packed hawker-style dishes and curries are served at communal cafe tables and accompanied by Thai-inflected cocktails. (☑03-9245 9800; www.bangpop.com.au; 35 South Wharf Promenade, South Wharf; mains $21-29; ⊙noon-late; 🍸; 🚋35, 70, 75)

Atlantic SEAFOOD $$$

10 🍴 Map p52, D3

'Simple sustainable seafood' is the mantra at this upmarket eatery in the casino complex. (☑03-9698 8888; www.theatlantic.com.au; Crown, Yarra Promenade, Southbank; mains $38-51; ⊙noon-3pm & 6-11pm; 🚋12, 96, 109)

CHAMELEONSEYE/SHUTTERSTOCK ©

Eureka Skydeck (p53)

Bistro Guillaume

FRENCH $$$

Sydney's famed Frenchman Guillaume Brahimi does bistro food at his Melbourne outpost (see 13 Map p52, D3) with fine-dining flair. (✆03-9292 4751; www.bistroguillaumemelbourne.com.au; Crown, Yarra Promenade, Southbank; mains $38-42; ⊗noon-late; 🚊55)

Colonial Tramcar Restaurant

BISTRO $$$

11 Map p52, C4

Dine in an elegant heritage tram as it rattles around the City Circle. Options include a four-course lunch, a three-course early dinner and a five-course late dinner, with drinks included in the price. The menus are simple, usually with a choice between chicken-breast or roast-beef mains; a separate vegetarian menu is available. (✆03-9695 4000; www.tramrestaurant.com.au; tram stop 125, Normanby Rd, Southbank; meals $82-140; ⊗departs 1pm, 5.45pm & 8.35pm; 🚊12, 96, 109)

Enlightened Cuisine

VEGETARIAN, CHINESE $$

12 Map p52, D4

Every imaginable variety of mock meat (generally made from wheat gluten or soy) is on offer here, served up in traditional Chinese style, from *kung pao* 'chicken' to king 'pork ribs' to buttered 'prawns'. All dishes are vegetarian and most can be made

Casino Dining

Crown (p53) has done a good job of luring people into its casino complex by installing some of Australia's most famous restaurateurs in glamorous riverside venues. While prices are steep, quality is high – unlike at some other eateries in this touristy stretch.

vegan on request. (☎03-9686 9188; 113 Queensbridge St, Southbank; mains $12-23; ⏱11.30am-2.30pm Mon, 11.30am-2.30pm & 5.30-10pm Tue-Sat, 5-10pm Sun; ✐; ⬜55)

Nobu

JAPANESE $$$

15 ❌ Map p52, D3

The jury's out on whether Melbourne really needed a Nobu in the first place, but it's a seductive space for those out to impress. (☎03-9292 7879; www.noburestaurants.com; Crown, Yarra Promenade, Southbank; dishes $29-64; ⏱noon-11pm; ⬜55)

Drinking

Ponyfish Island

BAR

14 ⬛ Map p52, E2

Not content with hiding bars down laneways or on rooftops, Melburnians are finding ever more creative spots to do their drinking. Where better than a little open-air nook on the pylon of a bridge arcing over the Yarra? It's a surprisingly good spot

to knock back beers while snacking on toasted sandwiches or cheese plates. (www.ponyfish.com.au; Southbank Pedestrian Bridge, Southbank; ⏱11am-late; ⬛Flinders St)

Boatbuilders Yard

BAR

15 ⬛ Map p52, C3

Occupying a slice of South Wharf next to the historic *Polly Woodside* ship, Boatbuilders attracts a mixed crowd of office workers, travellers and Melburnians keen to discover this developing area. It's made up of 'zones' running seamlessly from the indoor cafe-bar to the outdoor BBQ and bocce pit. There are usually live bands or DJs at weekends. (☎03-9686 5088; www.theboatbuildersyard.com.au; 23 South Wharf Promenade, South Wharf; ⏱7am-late; ⬜12, 96, 109)

Entertainment

Melbourne Theatre Company

THEATRE

16 ⭐ Map p52, E3

Melbourne's major theatrical company stages around a dozen productions each year, ranging from contemporary (including many new Australian works) to Shakespeare and other classics. Performances take place in its award-winning Southbank Theatre, a striking black building enclosed within angular white tubing. (MTC; ☎03-8688 0800; www.mtc.com.au; 140 Southbank Blvd, Southbank; ⬜1)

Australian Ballet

BALLET

17 ⭐ Map p52, E3

More than 50 years old, the Melbourne-based Australian Ballet performs traditional and new works in the Arts Centre and all around the country. You can take an hour-long tour of the Primrose Potter Australian Ballet Centre ($39, bookings essential) that includes a visit to the production and wardrobe departments as well as watching the dancers practise in the studios. (☏1300 369 741; www.australianballet.com.au; 2 Kavanagh St, Southbank; 🚊1)

Melbourne Recital Centre

CLASSICAL MUSIC

18 ⭐ Map p52, E3

This building may look like a framed piece of giant honeycomb, but it's actually the home (or hive?) where the Melbourne Chamber Orchestra (www.mco.org.au) and lots of other small ensembles regularly perform. Its two halls are said to have some of the best acoustics in the southern hemisphere. Performances range from chamber music to contemporary classical, jazz, world music and dance. (☏03-9699 3333; www.melbournerecital.com.au; 31 Sturt St, Southbank; ⊙box office 9am-5pm Mon-Fri; ☎; 🚊1)

Hamer Hall

CONCERT VENUE

19 ⭐ Map p52, E3

Part of Arts Centre Melbourne (p53), this large, round structure is well known for its excellent acoustics, with decor inspired by Australia's mineral and gemstone deposits. It's the home of the Melbourne Symphony Orchestra (p57), and the Australian Chamber Orchestra (www.aco.com.au) also plays here regularly. (☏1300 182 183; www.artscentremelbourne.com.au; 100 St Kilda Rd, Southbank; 🚊1, 3, 6, 16, 64, 67, 72, 🚉Flinders St)

Melbourne Symphony Orchestra

LIVE PERFORMANCE

The MSO has a broad reach: while not afraid to be populist (it's done

Understand
Bunjil

As you drive through Docklands or catch a train through Southern Cross station, you can't miss *Eagle*. Let's just say this bird has presence. Local sculptor Bruce Armstrong was inspired by the figure of Bunjil, the Wurundjeri creator spirit. The cast-aluminium bird rests contentedly on a mammoth jarrah perch, confidently surveying all around with a serene, glassy gaze. He's a reminder of the wordless natural world, scaled to provide a gentle parody of the surrounding cityscape's attempted domination.

sell-out performances with Burt Bacharach and Kiss), it usually performs classical symphonic master works. It plays regularly at its Hamer Hall home (see 19 ⭐ Map p52, E3), but it also has a summer series of free concerts at the Sidney Myer Music Bowl. (MSO; 📞03-9929 9600; www.mso.com.au)

Chunky Move
DANCE

20 ⭐ Map p52, E4

This acclaimed contemporary-dance company performs mainly at the Malthouse Theatre (p58). It also runs a variety of public dance classes; check the website. (📞03-9645 5188; www.chunkymove.com.au; 111 Sturt St, Southbank; 🚊1)

Malthouse Theatre
THEATRE

21 ⭐ Map p52, E4

Dedicated to promoting Australian works, this exciting company stages interesting productions in its own theatre, converted from an atmospheric old brick malthouse. (📞03-9685 5111; www.malthousetheatre.com.au; 113 Sturt St, Southbank; 🚊1)

Top Tip

Arts Centre

Whether or not you're interested in seeing a show, it's worth calling into Arts Centre Melbourne (p53), as there are often excellent free exhibitions in the gallery of the Theatres Building.

Etihad Stadium
STADIUM

22 ⭐ Map p52, B2

This easy-to-access Docklands stadium seats around 50,000 people for regular AFL games and the odd one-day cricket match, Rugby Union test and Justin Bieber concert – with the advantage of a retractable roof to keep spectators dry. Also runs tours for sporting tragics. (📞tours 03-8625 7277; www.etihadstadium.com.au; 740 Bourke St, Docklands; tours adult/child $15/8; 🚉Southern Cross)

Victorian Opera
OPERA

Dedicated to innovation and accessibility, this opera company's program, pleasingly, doesn't always play it safe. It performs mainly at Arts Centre Melbourne (p53) and the Melbourne Recital Centre (p57). (📞03-9001 6400; www.victorianopera.com.au)

Shopping

NGV Design Store
DESIGN

23 🔒 Map p52, E3

This large store sells well-designed and thoughtful show-based merchandise, arty T-shirts, a beautifully produced range of posters, and a hefty collection of art and design books. (📞03-8620 2243; www.ngv.vic.gov.au; NGV International, 180 St Kilda Rd, Southbank; ⊙10am-5pm; 🚉Flinders St)

Etihad Stadium

DFO South Wharf

MALL

24 🔒 Map p52, B3

Set over two floors, this large centre offers factory-outlet shopping at its most tempting. Big brands represented include Ben Sherman, Tumi, Lacoste, Victoria's Secret, Vans and Converse. (www.dfo.com.au; 20 Convention Centre Pl, South Wharf; ⊙10am-6pm Sat-Thu, to 9pm Fri; 🚌12, 96, 109)

Local Life
Williamstown

A trip over the Westgate Bridge brings you to the seaside suburb of Williamstown, a yacht-filled gem with an historic, salty seafaring atmosphere. In what is one of Melbourne's oldest settlements you'll find plenty of charming 18th-century architecture. It has stunning cityscape views of Melbourne best enjoyed while arriving by ferry, the most popular and fitting way, given the area's maritime ambience.

Getting There

⚓ Williamstown Ferries and Melbourne River Cruises arrive at Gem Pier.

🚆 Williamstown line departs from Flinders Street Station.

🚴 Hobsons Bay Coastal Trail links up with the Maribyrnong trail via the city.

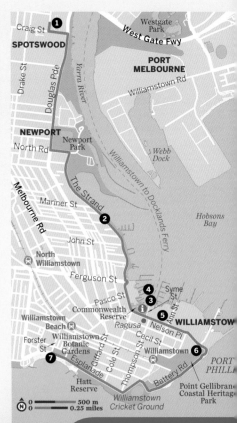

❶ Scienceworks

Incorporating an old brick sewage-pumping station that resembles a French chateau, **Scienceworks** (✆13 11 02; www.museumvictoria.com.au/science works; 2 Booker St, Spotswood; adult/child $14/free, plus Planetarium & Lightning Room $10/6; ◷10am-4.30pm; ⊞Spotswood) keeps inquisitive grey matter occupied with interactive displays. The planetarium splashes the universe onto a 16m-domed ceiling during 40-minute shows.

❷ Waterfront Promenade

Williamstown's main strip hugs the harbourfront, making it the place to soak up seaside charm. Here you'll find historic shopfronts, bluestone pubs and a park overlooking the bay to eat fish and chips in. Or pop into **Ragusa** (✆03-9399 8500; www.ragusares taurant.com.au; 139 Nelson Pl, Williamstown; mains $29-50; ◷noon-3pm & 6pm-late Tue-Sun; ⊞; ⊞Williamstown) for modern Croatian set in a heritage building.

❸ Gem Pier

Williamstown's centrepiece is the ferry arrival point, a sparkling marina surrounded by bobbing yachts and sensational city views. The **Hobsons Bay Visitor Information Centre** (✆03-9932 4310; www.visithobsonsbay.com.au; cnr Syme St & Nelson Pl, Williamstown; ◷9am-5pm, tours 11.45am Tue & Fri Mar-May & Sep-Nov; ⊞Williamstown) should be your first stop for free historical walking tours in autumn and spring.

❹ HMAS Castlemaine

Also at Gem Pier, take a look around the last of 60 Australian-built Bathurst Class corvettes still afloat. The **HMAS Castlemaine** (✆03-9397 2363; www.hmas castlemaine.org.au; Gem Pier, Williamstown; adult/child $6/3; ◷noon-4pm Sat & Sun; ⊞Williamstown) did time as an escort ship and minesweeper during WWII.

❺ Seaworks & Sea Shepherd

The industrial **Seaworks** (✆0417 292 021; www.seaworks.com.au; 82 Nelson Pl, Williamstown; ◷8am-8pm Nov-Mar, to 6pm Apr-Oct; ⊞Williamstown) comprises historic boat sheds, a maritime museum, a pirate-themed tavern and Victoria's oldest morgue (1859; visit on a ghost tour). It's also the headquarters for anti-whaling campaigners Sea Shepherd Australia. It's often possible to drop by and tour its vessels – check the website for tour times.

❻ Point Gellibrand

The site of Victoria's first white settlement, Point Gellibrand's where Victoria's navy was established, and where the Timeball Tower, once used by ships to set their chronometers, was built by convict labour in 1840.

❼ Williamstown Beach

Forget St Kilda – the pleasant lopsided grin of coarse golden sand at **Williamstown Beach** (Esplanade, Williamstown; ⊞Williamstown Beach) is a much more appealing place for a dip. It has its own surf-lifesaving club, a swimming pool down one end and a pavilion at the other.

Explore

South Melbourne, Port Melbourne & Albert Park

The well-heeled trio of South Melbourne, Port Melbourne and Albert Park isn't short on lunching ladies or AFL stars living it up in grandiose Victorian terraces and bayside condos. Leafy and generally sedate, the area boasts some of Melbourne's most beautiful heritage architecture. South Melbourne is the busiest neighbourhood, with a bustling market.

The Sights in a Day

☀ Set off midmorning to **South Melbourne Market** (p66) and grab a coffee at **Clement** (p70) or **Padre Coffee** (p70) – and a sneaky dim sim, an institution here. Then work it off with a stroll around the picturesque streets and over to **Station Pier** (p68) in Port Melbourne to observe the harbour activity and maybe even take a brisk swim at one of the city bay beaches.

☀ Make your way to **Albert Park Lake** (p67) for more exercise walking around the Formula One street circuit. Then shop at the boutique stores, check out the classic architecture at **St Vincent Place** (p66) and sample a classic Australian-style burger with the lot at **Andrew's** (p69). Have a walk around **Gasworks Arts Park** (p68), taking in the galleries and open-air sculptures.

☽ Head back to South Melbourne for the some of the tastiest paella at **Simply Spanish** (p68) or tuck into Italian washed down with some excellent wine at **Bellota Wine Bar** (p68).

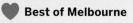 **Best of Melbourne**

Eating

St Ali (p68)

Jock's Ice-Cream (p69)

Shopping

Avenue Books (p70)

Getting There

🚋 **Tram** All three neighbourhoods are well served by trams. From the city, tram 109 runs parallel to Port Melbourne's main shopping strip, Bay St, terminating at Station Pier. Tram 12 runs along South Melbourne's main shopping strip and both it and tram 96 are handy for South Melbourne Market. Tram 1 crosses Clarendon St on its way to Albert Park and the beach.

For reviews see
- Sights p66
- Eating p68
- Drinking p70
- Shopping p70

E
F
G
H

West Gate Fwy

Whiteman St
City Rd
Kings Way
Sturt St

Chessell St
Market St
Ross St
York St
Moray St
Coventry St
1

St Kilda Rd
11

South Melbourne Market
1
8
Eastern Rd
Tope St

York St
Ferrars St
Cecil St
15 14
Dorcas St
Park St
Kings Way

Montague St
Dorcas St
Bank St
Clarendon St
Bank St
7
Park St
Stead St
2

SOUTH MELBOURNE

Dow St
Napier St
Cobden St
Raglan St
Thomson St
Albert Rd

Park St
Draper St
St Vincent Pl N
St Vincent Place
Anzac Gardens
Martin St
Cecil St
Church St
Albert Rd Dr
Lakeside Dr
3

St Vincent Pl N
St Vincent Gardens
St Vincent Pl S
2
Bevan St
Bridport St
Ferrars St
Albert Rd
Lakeside Stadium
Gunn Island

Brooke St
Dundas Pl
Albert Park Lake
4
Albert Park Golf Course
4

Cardigan Pl
13
10
Victoria Ave
O'Grady St
Montague St
Finlay St
Kerferd Rd
Melbourne Sports & Aquatic Centre
Lakeside Dr

ALBERT PARK

Merton St
Herbert St
Albert Park
Albert Park Lake

Richardson St
Simpson St
Carter St
Hambleton St
Erskine St
Richardson St
Harold St
Canterbury Rd
Aughtie Dr

Kerferd Rd
Page St
Little Page St
Danks St
Mills St
MIDDLE PARK
5

Sights

South Melbourne Market

MARKET

1 ◎ Map p64, E2

Trading since 1864, this market is a neighbourhood institution, its labyrinthine guts packed with a brilliant collection of stalls selling everything from organic produce and deli treats to hipster specs, art and crafts. The place is famous for its dim sims (sold here since 1949), and there's no shortage of atmospheric eateries. From early January to late February, there's a lively night market on Thursday. The site is also home to a cooking school – see the website for details. (☑03-9209 6295; www.southmelbournemarket.com.au; cnr Coventry & Cecil Sts, South Melbourne; ◷8am-4pm Wed, Sat & Sun, to 5pm Fri; 🚋12, 96)

St Vincent Place

ARCHITECTURE

2 ◎ Map p64, E3

For a taste of Victorian-era finery, take a stroll in St Vincent Pl, a heritage precinct in Albert Park. Consisting of a long, arch-shaped street skirting a central landscaped garden, it's considered Australia's finest example of a 19th-century residential square. The street itself is flanked by some of Melbourne's grandest Victorian terraces, many of which date to the 1860s. Such elegance and boldness reflect Melbourne's blooming confidence during the gold rush. The precinct is 700m south of South Melbourne Market. (St Vincent Pl, Albert Park; 🚋1)

Albert Park Golf Course

GOLF

3 ◎ Map p64, H4

This 18-hole championship golf course is set on the fringes of Albert Park Lake, just 2km from the city. Located alongside the Australian

---

Understand
Australian Formula One Grand-Prix

These are the kind of figures that make petrol-heads swoon: 300km/h, 950bhp and 19,000rpm. The Australian Grand Prix is held at Albert Park's 5.3km street circuit, which winds around the normally tranquil park's lake and is known for its smooth, fast surface. The buzz, both on the streets and in your ears, takes over Melbourne for four days in March, attracting 110,000 spectators for race day. Since 2009 it's been a twilight race, starting at 5pm (mainly for the benefit of TV audiences in the European time zones). Visit www.grandprix.com.au for event and ticketing details.

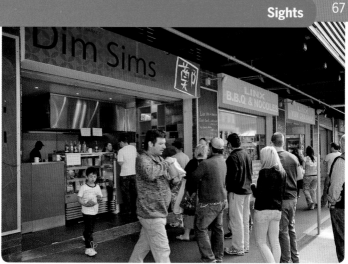

South Melbourne Market

Formula One Grand Prix racing circuit, a separate driving range (www.albertparkdrivingrange.com. au) allows golfers to hit off from 65 two-tier all-weather bays. (☑03-9510 5588; www.albertparkgolf.com.au; Queens Rd, Albert Park; 18 holes weekdays/weekend $34/39, driving range 50/100 balls $9.90/17.90; ☺golf course dawn-dusk, driving range 10am-10pm Mon, 7am-10pm Tue-Fri, 7am-9pm Sat & Sun; ☐3, 5, 6, 16, 64, 67)

Albert Park Lake LAKE

4 ◉ Map p64, H4

Elegant black swans give their inimitable bottoms-up salute as you jog, cycle or walk the 5km perimeter of this constructed lake. Lakeside Dr was used as an international motor-racing circuit in the 1950s, and since 1996 the revamped track has been the venue for the **Australian Formula One Grand Prix** (☑1800 100 030; www.grandprix.com.au; tickets from $55; ☺Mar) each March. Also on the periphery is the **Melbourne Sports & Aquatic Centre** (MSAC; ☑03-9926 1555; www.msac.com.au; Albert Rd; adult/child from $8.20/5.60; ☺5.30am-10pm Mon-Fri, 7am-8pm Sat & Sun; ☐96, 112), with an Olympic-size pool and child-delighting wave machine. (btwn Queens Rd, Fitzroy St, Aughtie Dr & Albert Rd; ☐96)

Gasworks Arts Park
ARTS CENTRE

5 ⊙ Map p64, D4

This former gas plant lay derelict from the 1950s before finding new purpose in life as an arts precinct, with red-brick galleries, a theatre company (check website for shows) and ultra-dog-friendly parkland. You can meet the artists on a guided tour or come for the farmers market (third Saturday of each month). The venue also hosts an open-air cinema season, usually in November. (☎03-8606 4200; www.gasworks.org.au; cnr Graham & Pickles St, Albert Park; tours adult/child $25/15; ⊙tours 10.30am & 2pm Mon-Thu; 🚋1, 109)

Station Pier
LANDMARK

6 ⊙ Map p64, A4

Melbourne's main sea terminal, Station Pier has great sentimental associations for many migrants who arrived by ship in the 1950s and '60s, as well as for service people who used it during WWII. It has been in operation since 1854, when the first major railway in Australia ran from here to the city. These days, it's where the *Spirit of Tasmania* ferry, cruise ships and navy vessels dock. (Waterfront Pl, Port Melbourne; 🚋109)

Eating

Bellota Wine Bar
ITALIAN $$$

7 ⊗ Map p64, F2

This handsome wine bar and bistro is an extension of the adjoining Prince Wine Store, with an ever-changing wine list and beautiful dishes to match. Whether you're dining at the bar or at one of the intimate back tables (the latter require a reservation), expect to swoon over perfect grilled octopus, *vitello tonnato* (thinly sliced veal) and elegant, nuanced pastas. (☎03-9078 8381; http://bellota.com.au; 181 Bank St, South Melbourne; mains $28-34; ⊙11am-11pm Tue-Sat; 🚋1, 12)

Simply Spanish
SPANISH $$

When a Melbourne restaurant wins the title of 'Best Paella Outside of Spain' in Valencia, you know you're on to a good thing. This casual market eatery (see 1 ⊙ Map p64, E2) is *the* place to go for paella, which is available here in numerous combos. While you wait, nibble on a tapas dish or two; the chilli-spiked garlic prawns are a top pick. (☎03-9682 6100; www.simplyspanish.com.au; South Melbourne Market, cnr Coventry & Cecil Sts, South Melbourne; gourmet paellas from $20.50, tapas $8-16; ⊙8am-9pm Wed-Sat, to 4pm Sun; 🚋12, 96)

St Ali
CAFE $

8 ⊗ Map p64, F1

A hideaway warehouse conversion where the coffee's carefully sourced and guaranteed to be good. If you can't decide between house blend, speciality, black or white, there's a six-coffee tasting 'adventure' ($20). The food menu covers all bases with competence and creativity, from virtuous vanilla-and-maple quinoa pudding with baby Thai basil to cult-status corn fritters with poached eggs and grilled halloumi. (☏03-9686 2990; www.stali.com.au; 12-18 Yarra Pl, South Melbourne; dishes $8-25; ◷7am-6pm; 🚊12)

Jock's Ice-Cream
ICE CREAM $

9 🍴 Map p64, E4

For almost two decades Jock has been scooping up his made-on-site sorbets and ice creams for baysiders (and the odd Canadian teen-pop icon). Cult-status flavours include hokey-pokey and a star-spangled jam-and-peanut-butter combo. Take-home tubs also available. (☏03-9686 3838; 83 Victoria Ave, Albert Park; single cone $4; ◷noon-8pm Mon-Thu, to 10pm Fri & Sat, to 9pm Sun; 🚊1)

Misuzu's
JAPANESE $$

10 🍴 Map p64, E4

Misuzu's menu includes whopping noodle, rice and curry dishes, tempuras and takeaway options from the neatly displayed sushi bar. Sit outside under a lantern-hung tree, or inside surrounded by murals and dark wood. (☏03-9699 9022; www.misuzus.com.au; 3-7 Victoria Ave, Albert Park; mains $17-32; ◷noon-10pm; 🚊1)

Orient East
MALAYSIAN $$

11 🍴 Map p64, H1

A convenient lunch spot if you're visiting the Shrine of Remembrance and Botanic Gardens across the road, Orient East whips up British-colonial Straits cuisine in a setting reminis-

cent of a 1960s foreign-correspondent cafe. Enjoy hawker-style grub such as black-pepper soft-shell-crab buns, prawn *char kuey teow* (fried flat noodles) and fragrant laksas, best washed down with some cold craft suds. (☏03-9685 2900; www.orienteast.com.au; 348 St Kilda Rd, Melbourne; mains $17-27; ◷6.30am-10pm Mon-Fri, 7-11am & 5-9pm Sat & Sun; 🚊3, 5, 6, 16, 64, 67, 72)

Paco y Lola
MEXICAN $$

Upbeat and casual, Paco y Lola (see 1 ◉ Map p64, E2) cooks up a storm of zingy, fresh, generous Mexican flavours, from juicy burritos, quesadillas and tacos to more substantial options like Mexican pork ribs and refreshing soft-shell-crab salad. If there are two of you, don't miss the *caldo de pescado*, a fragrant Mexican fish soup made with super-fresh seafood from the adjoining market. (📞03-9696 5659; http://pacoylola.com.au; Shop 99, South Melbourne Market, cnr Coventry & Cecil Sts, South Melbourne; burritos $13-14, mains $15-30; 🕒8.30am-10.30pm Wed & Fri, 9am-11pm Thu, 7.30am-11pm Sat, 7.30am-5pm Sun; 🚌12, 96)

Drinking

Clement
CAFE

There's a buzz about this tiny cafe (see 1 ◉ Map p64, E2) on the perimeter of South Melbourne Market, not only for its expertly crafted brew but also for its homemade salted-caramel or jam-and-custard doughnuts. Grab a streetside stool or get a takeaway and wander the market stalls. (www.clementcoffee.com; Shop 89, South Melbourne Market, cnr Coventry & Cecil Sts, South Melbourne; 🕒7am-5pm; 🚌12, 96)

✅ Top Tip
Market Walking Tour
To dig deeper into the riches of South Melbourne Market (p66), join one of the market's appetite-piquing walking tours ($10). Run on the third Saturday of the month at 10am, the 90-minute tours shed light on the site's history as well as its current vendors (yes, food sampling is involved!). Tours can be booked on the market website.

Colonial Brewery Co
BREWERY

12 🍺 Map p64, B1

This east coast outpost of Western Australian craft brewery Colonial pours smooth, thirst-crushing suds in a huge warehouse decked out with steel tanks, ping-pong table and food trucks. Staff are passionate and knowledgeable about the beers (which include seasonal drops), and the Kolsch goes down especially well. (📞03-8644 4044; www.colonialbrewingco.com.au/port-melbourne; 89 Bertie St, Port Melbourne; 🕒noon-11pm Thu & Fri; 🚌109)

Padre Coffee
CAFE

Padre Coffee (see 1 ◉ Map p64, E2) Offers a perfect (and popular) caffeine-enhanced respite from mad market shopping. (📞03-9699 8348; www.padrecoffee.com.au; shop 33, South Melbourne Market, Cnr Coventry & Cecil Sts, South Melbourne; 🕒8am-4pm Wed, Fri, Sat & Sun; 🚌12, 96)

Shopping

Avenue Books
BOOKS

13 🔒 Map p64, E4

Everyone needs a neighbourhood bookshop like this one, full of nooks and crannies to perch with literary fiction, cooking, gardening, art and children's books. Cluey staff make spot-on recommendations too. (📞03-9690 2227; www.avenuebookstore.com.au; 127 Dundas Pl, Albert Park; 🕒9am-7pm; 🚌1)

Station Pier (p68)

Coventry Bookstore
BOOKS

14 🔒 Map p64, F2

Despite its modest size, this independent trader packs a punch with a clued-up selection of books. Lose track of time while leafing through local and international fiction and biographies, not to mention beautiful tomes on travel, design, fashion, architecture and more. Little bookworms will appreciate the dedicated children's book room out the back. (📞03-9686 8200; www.coventrybookstore. com.au; 265 Coventry St, South Melbourne; ⏰9.30am-5.30pm Mon-Fri, 9am-5pm Sat, 9.30am-4.30pm Sun; 🚊1, 12)

Nest
HOMEWARES

15 🔒 Map p64, F2

In a soothing, light-filled space, Nest stocks a gorgeous range of homewares and gifts, from 100%-linen bedding to soy candles, Aesop skincare and a range of cotton-knit 'comfort wear' that's way too nice to hide at home in. Staff are delightful. From South Melbourne Market head along Coventry St. (📞03-9699 8277; www. nesthomewares.com.au; 289 Coventry St, South Melbourne; ⏰9.30am-5.30pm Mon-Sat, to 5pm Sun; 🚊12, 96)

South Yarra, Prahran & Windsor

South Yarra, Prahran and Windsor are Melbourne's cool kids: fashion obsessed, body conscious and party loving. While the South Yarra end of Chapel St has sold its soul to high-street chains, the Prahran and Windsor end rocks with of-the-moment eateries, bars, boutiques and street art that pull trendy, eye-candy crowds. Kissing South Yarra's northwestern edge is Melbourne's showpiece Botanic Gardens.

The Sights in a Day

☀ Start with breakfast at **Gilson** (p80) before heading across to the **Royal Botanic Gardens** (p74). Stroll the grounds, feed the ducks and make your way through the park to pay your respects at the **Shrine of Remembrance** (p78), a monumental building dedicated to Australians at war. Book an appointment afterwards to tour the contemporary art collection at **Justin Art House Museum.** (p78)

☀ Then its time to venture into Prahran, starting at **Prahran Market** (p81) to browse fresh produce and gourmet food, and maybe sign up for a cooking class. Grab a top notch coffee at **Market Lane** (p82), before hitting Chapel St for some serious shopping: for brand names and high-end boutiques go to the South Yarra end, for vintage and secondhand clothes head towards Windsor

☾ There's plenty going on at night, with a huge choice of quality restaurants and nightlife at your fingers. Choose creative Thai dishes at **Colonel Tan's** (p80), or go upmarket at **Woodland House** (p80) – if you've booked well in advance. Be sure to save room for a dessert to remember at **Zumbo** (p80). Head to swanky **Rufus** (p82) for cocktails or rock 'n' roll lovin' **Yellow Bird** (p84) to finish off the night.

👁 **Top Sights**

Royal Botanic Gardens (p74)

💗 **Best of Melbourne**

Eating

Woodland House (p80)

Zumbo (p80)

Drinking

Rufus (p82)

Yellow Bird (p84)

Market Lane (p82)

Getting There

🚆 **Train** South Yarra station is served by Sandringham-, Frankston- and Dandenong-line trains. Both Prahran and Windsor stations are on the Sandringham line.

🚋 **Tram** From the city, trams 3, 5, 6, 16, 64, 67 and 72 reach the Shrine of Remembrance (and adjoining Royal Botanic Gardens).

Top Sights
Royal Botanic Gardens

Melbourne's Royal Botanic Gardens is simply glorious. From the air, the gardens' 94-acre spread evokes a giant green lung in the middle of the city. Drawing over 1.5 million visitors annually, the gardens is considered one of the finest examples of Victorian-era landscaping in the world. Take a book, picnic or Frisbee – but, most importantly, take your time.

Map p76, A1

www.rbg.vic.gov.au

Birdwood Ave, South Yarra

admission free

7.30am-sunset

Tourist Shuttle, 1, 3, 5, 6, 16, 64, 67, 72

Water feature, Royal Botanic Gardens

Flora Collections

The gardens is home to over 10,000 native and introduced plant species, displayed in a number of collections. On hot days, the lush, primordial Fern Gully offers cooling relief, while the striking Guilfoyle's Volcano is not really a volcano but a restored 19th-century reservoir. The gardens' centrepiece is the Ornamental Lake, which, like Fern Gully, is a relic of a lake system that predates the city's European settlement.

Observatory

Just outside Gate D is the **Melbourne Observatory** (✆03-9252 2429; adult/child/family $24/20/70; ⏲tours by appointment 9pm Mon). On Monday evening the observatory runs tours of the complex, which still uses much of its original astrological hardware. Tours are run by experienced guides from the Astronomical Society of Victoria. Bookings are obligatory and can be made via the 'What's On' section of the gardens' website.

Ian Potter Foundation Children's Garden

At the gardens' western entrance is this award-winning **children's garden** (✆03-9252 2300; www.rbg.vic.gov.au/visit-melbourne/attractions/children-garden; ⏲10am-dusk Wed-Sun, daily Victorian school holidays). Interactive play areas include a Tree Tower, a Ruin Garden, a Bamboo Forest and a Kitchen Garden. If the weather's warm, pack your little ones' swimwear and let them loose at the splash-happy spiral fountains (operating till 4pm).

Alfresco Film & Theatre

From early December to early April, the gardens play host to **Moonlight Cinema** (www.moonlight.com.au), a season of alfresco film screenings ranging from current mainstream releases to cult and classic flicks. Bring your own picnic hamper or buy light eats and booze at the venue.

☑ Top Tips

▶ A range of guided tours depart from the visitor centre by Gate D; a highlight is the Aboriginal Heritage Walk.

▶ The gardens play host to theatre performances during summer; check the website to see what's on.

▶ Pack a picnic blanket, a hat and sunscreen in case the shaded areas are taken.

✗ Take a Break

You'll find French-Vietnamese cafe Jardin Tan beside the visitor centre at Gate D and The Terrace cafe by the gardens' Ornamental Lake. While both are fine for a coffee pit stop, an altogether better option for food and drinks is Gilson (p80), a quick walk from Gate E at the southern end of the gardens.

For reviews see
- ◉ Top Sights   p74
- ⊙ Sights   p78
- ⊗ Eating   p80
- ⦿ Drinking   p82
- ⊛ Shopping   p85

Sights

Justin Art House Museum
GALLERY

1 Map p76, E8

Book ahead for a private tour of Melbourne art collectors Charles and Leah Justin's dynamic collection of contemporary art, consisting of more than 250 pieces amassed over four decades. There's a strong emphasis on video and digital art, with the works rotated regularly. Guided tours take around two hours. (JAHM; ☑0411 158 967; www.jahm.com.au; cnr Williams Rd & Lumley Ct, Prahran; adult/child $25/free; ⊘by appointment; ☒5, 6, 64)

Shrine of Remembrance
MONUMENT

2 Map p76, A2

One of Melbourne's icons, the Shrine of Remembrance is a commanding memorial to Victorians killed in WWI. Built between 1928 and 1934,

much of it with Depression-relief, or 'susso' (sustenance), labour, its stoic, classical design is partly based on the Mausoleum of Halicarnassus, one of the seven ancient wonders of the world. The shrine's upper balcony affords epic panoramic views of the Melbourne skyline and all the way up tram-studded Swanston St. (☑03-9661 8100; www.shrine.org.au; Birdwood Ave, South Yarra; admission free; ⊘10am-5pm; ☒Tourist Shuttle, ☒3, 5, 6, 16, 64, 67, 72)

Como House
HISTORIC BUILDING

3 Map p76, E3

A wedding cake of Australian Regency and Italianate architecture, this elegant colonial residence is among Melbourne's heritage royalty. Dating to 1840, it houses numerous belongings of the high-society Armytage family, the last and longest owners, who lived in the house for 95 years. House tours run every Saturday and Sunday and tickets can be purchased online or by phone. (☑03-9827 2500, tour bookings 03-9656 9889; www.nationaltrust.org.au; cnr Williams Rd & Lechlade Ave, South Yarra; adult/child/family $15/9/35; ⊘gardens 9am-5pm Mon-Sat, from 10am Sun, house tours 11am, 12.30pm & 2pm Sat & Sun; ☒58)

Government House
HISTORIC BUILDING

4 Map p76, A2

On the outer edge of the Botanic Gardens, the Italianate Government House dates to 1872. A replica of Queen Victoria's Osborne House on

LEONARD ZHUKOVSKY/SHUTTERSTOCK ©

Government House

England's Isle of Wight, it has served as the residence of all Victorian governors, as well as being the royal pied-à-terre. Unfortunately, the two-hour tour of the property is only available to groups of 10 or more. Tours should be booked at least two weeks ahead, by phone or email. (☏03-9656 9889; www.nationaltrust.org.au; Kings Domain, South Yarra; tours $18; ⊙tours 10am Mon & Thu; ☐Tourist Shuttle, ☐1, 3, 5, 6, 16, 58, 64, 67, 72)

Herring Island   PARK

5 ◎ Map p76, E2

This prelapsarian river island is a sanctuary for the Yarra's original trees, grasses and indigenous animals. Within is an impressive collection of environmental sculpture, including work by Brit Andy Goldsworthy and numerous Australian artists, among them Julie Collins, Robert Jacks, Robert Bridgewater, John Davis and Ellen José. There are designated picnic and BBQ areas. On summer weekends, a Parks Victoria punt operates from Como Landing on Alexandra Ave in South Yarra; at other times you'll need a kayak to get here. (http://parkweb.vic.gov.au/explore/parks/herring-island; Alexandra Ave, South Yarra; ☐605, ☐78)

Eating

Zumbo
DESSERTS $

6 ✗ Map p76, C3

Aussie pâtissier Adriano Zumbo is hot property, famed for his outrageously creative, technically ambitious concoctions. Here, cheesecake might be made with yuzu-cream-cheese mousse and shaped like a Swiss cheese, and a tart might get spicy with churros-custard crème and Mexican-hot-chocolate crème. And then there's the '70s disco-chamber-like fit-out. Fine print: the coffee's better next door. (📞1800 858 611; http://zumbo.com.au; 14 Claremont St, South Yarra; macarons $2.80, cakes from $6; ⏰7am-7pm; 🚌58, 78, 🚉South Yarra)

Woodland House
MODERN AUSTRALIAN $$$

7 ✗ Map p76, E7

In a glorious Victorian villa, Woodland House is home turf for young-gun chefs Thomas Woods and Hayden McFarland, former sous chefs for lauded Melbourne restaurateur Jacques Reymond. The menu spotlights quality local produce, cooked confidently and creatively in dishes like wood-roasted mussels with asparagus and salted yolk. Thursday and Friday offer a good-value three-course lunch with a glass of wine for $55. (📞03-9525 2178; www.woodlandhouse.com.au; 78 Williams Rd, Prahran; tasting menus from $125; ⏰6.30-9pm Tue, Wed & Sat, noon-3pm & 6.30-9pm Thu & Fri, noon-3pm Sun; 🚌6)

Da Noi
ITALIAN $$$

8 ✗ Map p76, B3

Elegant Da Noi serves up beautiful dishes from Sardinia, the island home of owner-chef Pietro Porcu. Offerings change daily, with the chef's special reinterpreted several times a night on some occasions. Just go with it. For the full effect, opt for the four-course set menu, which sees the chef decide your dishes based on whatever's best that day. Bookings advised. (📞03-9866 5975; http://danoi.com.au; 95 Toorak Rd, South Yarra; mains $30-40, 4-course tasting menu $75-95; ⏰noon-10.30pm; 🚌58, 🚉South Yarra)

Gilson
MODERN AUSTRALIAN $$

9 ✗ Map p76, A2

Sassy new kid Gilson straddles the line between cafe and restaurant. Directly opposite the Botanic Gardens, it has a concrete and Italian-marble fit-out inspired by midcentury French modernism and contemporary, Italian-influenced food. Forgo the famous (and underwhelming) grilled cucumber for the outstanding pasta dishes and interesting wood-fired pizzas. Rounding things off are intriguing wines and cocktails, and attentive, knowledgeable staff. (📞03-9866 3120; http://gilsonrestaurant.com.au; 171 Domain Rd, South Yarra; pizzas $18-25, mains $24-34; ⏰6am-11pm Mon-Fri, from 7am Sat & Sun; 🚌58)

Colonel Tan's
THAI $$

In the back corner of pumping Revolver Upstairs (p85), retro-licious Colonel Tan (see 23 🗺 Map p76, C6) has dishes out top-notch Thai-American fusion. Expect such things as corn, coriander and pickled-chilli doughnuts, soft-shell-crab burgers with curried egg, and a Bangkok bolognese that tastes a hell of a lot better than it sounds. (📞03-9521 5985; http://revolverupstairs. com.au/colonel-tans; 229 Chapel St, Prahran; mains $15-29; ⏰5-11pm Tue-Thu & Sat, from noon Fri; 🚌6, 78, 🚆Prahran)

Drugstore Espresso
CAFE $

10 🍴 Map p76, C4

A split-level, graffiti-pimped hipster haven, Drugstore trades in serious coffee and smashing brekky and lunchtime grub. Lick your whiskers over buttermilk hotcakes with maple bacon, stone fruit and whipped espresso ricotta, or lunch on canned sardines with sourdough, local stracciatella cheese, heirloom tomatoes, basil, chilli oil, fried capers and poached egg. It's Toorak Rd, Jim, but not as we know it. (📞03-9827 5058; www.drugstoreespresso.com.au; 194 Toorak Rd, South Yarra; dishes $15-22; ⏰7am-4pm Mon-Fri, 8am-4pm Sat & Sun; 🛜; 🚌58, 78, 🚆South Yarra)

Fonda
MEXICAN $$

11 🍴 Map p76, C7

Fun, thumping Fonda serves Mexican-with-a-twist street food. The emphasis is on fresh, local ingredients, from Queen Vic Market produce to authentic, made-from-scratch tacos. Order the prawn taco with kimchi and caramelised pineapple and wash it down with a burnt-orange margarita. Dine downstairs or try your luck on the rooftop (ridiculously busy at weekends). (📞03-9521 2660; http://fondamexican.com.au; 144 Chapel St, Windsor; tacos from $6.50, burritos from $14; ⏰11.30am-10.30pm Sun-Thu, to 11pm Fri & Sat, rooftop from 5.30pm Mon-Wed, from noon Thu-Sun; 🚌6, 78, 🚆Windsor)

Hawker Hall
SOUTHEAST ASIAN $$

12 🍴 Map p76, C7

Did you hear the one about the turn-of-the-century stable turned hipster take

🔍 Local Life
Prahran Market

Prahran Market (📞03-8290 8220; www.prahranmarket.com.au; 163 Commercial Rd, South Yarra; ⏰7am-5pm Tue & Thu-Sat, 10am-3pm Sun; 🚌72, 78, 🚆Prahran) is a Melbourne institution, whetting appetites since 1881. While much of the current structure dates to the 1970s and '80s, the Commercial Rd facade – designed by Charles D'Ebro in a Queen Anne–revival style – dates to 1891. Grab a speciality coffee from Market Lane and trawl stalls heaving with organic produce, seafood, meat, handmade pasta, gourmet deli items and more. The market is also home to culinary store and cooking school Essential Ingredient.

on a Southeast Asian food hall? Decked with playful Chinatown-style signage, ever-popular Hawker Hall serves up spicy, punchy share-style dishes like barbecue pork and lychee salad and fiery Portuguese devil chicken curry. No reservations, so head in before 6pm or after 9.30pm to minimise the wait. (☏03-8560 0090; http://hawkerhall.com.au; 98 Chapel St, Windsor; dishes $8-34; ☺11am-late; 🚌5, 6, 64, 78, 🚊Windsor)

Two Birds One Stone CAFE $

13 ⊗ Map p76, C3

Sandblasted oak stools, whitewashed timber and a wintry forest mural evoke Scandinavia at Two Birds One Stone, a crisp, contemporary cafe with smooth third-wave coffee and a smart, produce-driven menu. Find your happy place tucking into soul-nourishing dishes like ricotta pancakes with figs, marmalade syrup and pistachio cream, or pan-seared salmon with potato rösti, truffled cauliflower puree and poached eggs. (☏03-9827 1228; www.twobirdsonestonecafe.com.au; 12 Claremont St, South Yarra; dishes $14-22.50; ☺7am-3.30pm Mon-Fri, from 8am Sat & Sun; 🚌58, 78, 🚊South Yarra)

Tivoli Road Bakery CAFE $

14 ⊗ Map p76, D3

Join fashionistas, realtors and upmarket hipsters at this contemporary, side-street bakery-cafe, serving everything from impossibly light custard doughnuts to generously stuffed sandwiches, made-from-scratch pies and sausage rolls, and fashionable

salads. Its cult-status artisanal loaves are also on offer, as well as a small selection of other local treats, from jam to nougat. (☏03-9041 4345; http://tiviroad.com.au; 3 Tivoli Rd, South Yarra; dishes $7-12; ☺7.30am-4pm; 🚌58, 78, 🚊South Yarra)

Drinking

Rufus COCKTAIL BAR

15 🚇 Map p76, C6

Hidden above Greville St, Rufus is deliciously posh and proper, dripping with chandeliers, tinted mirrors and swagged drapes. That the place is named after Sir Winston Churchill's beloved poodle is no coincidence: the late British prime minister is Rufus' muse, hence the emphasis on quality champagnes, martinis and whiskies, the standout Yorkshire-pudding roll, and your butlerlike waiter. Enter from the laneway. (☏03-9525 2197; www.rufusbar.com.au; 1st fl, 143 Greville St, Prahran; ☺4pm-late; 🚌6, 72, 78, 🚊Prahran)

Market Lane Coffee CAFE

16 🚇 Map p76, C5

This is one of Melbourne's top speciality coffee roasters, hiding away at the back of Prahran Market. The beans here are strictly seasonal, producing cups of joe that are beautifully nuanced...and best paired with one of the scrumptious pastries. Free one-hour cuppings run at 10am on

Understand

The Coffee Capital

Cafes are an integral part of daily Victorian life. Many Melburnians are up early so they can catch up with colleagues or just the newspaper over a latte and a slice of sourdough before the workday begins, and weekends see cafes fill up fast (lengthy queues are not uncommon) with those looking for a long, leisurely, blow-out breakfast.

The cafe tradition goes back to the early years of last century, with the arrival of Victoria's first wave of Italian and Greek migrants, but really took off post-WWII when large numbers of Italians settled in the inner city and the first Gaggia and La Cimbali espresso machines were imported under licence in 1953. Bourke St's Pellegrini's (p40) is an ever-enchanting survivor of this generation. The brew in its signature Duralex glasses may be unremarkable by today's standards, but the Italian brio, urban bonhomie and original decor are as authentic as it gets. Melbourne *torrefazione* (Italian coffee roasters) such as Genovese and Grinders also date back to this era, and their bean blends now fuel cafes all over the country. Other long-term local roasters include Atomic, Jasper and Gravity.

While these original family-run roasters have prospered and become household names, Melbourne is now firmly in the grip of coffee's third wave. Coffee talk now runs to *terroir*, and single-origin beans, premium small-batch roasts and alternative brewing methods such as siphon, pour-over, filter and cold-drip have taken coffee appreciation to a new level. Melbourne is in an era of extreme coffee excellence.

Third-wave pioneer Mark Dundon owns Seven Seeds (p133) – part cafe, part retail outlet and part instructional facility, set in a warehouse conversion that wins in both the sustainability and style stakes. He also runs city cafes Brother Baba Budan and Traveller. Salvatore Malatesta took over South Melbourne's legendary St Ali (p68) from Dundon, and now also runs a stable of other cafes. Other third-wavers doing great things include Market Lane (p82) at Prahran Market, Industry Beans (p113) in Fitzroy, Lygon St's Padre Coffee (p101), and Proud Mary (p112) in Collingwood.

Saturday (get in by 9.30am to secure your place). (📞03-9804 7434; www.marketlane.com.au; Prahran Market, 163 Commercial Rd, South Yarra; ⏱7am-5pm Tue & Thu-Sat, to 4pm Wed, 8am-5pm Sun; 🚌72, 78, 79, 🚊Prahran)

Woods of Windsor
BAR

17 🍺 Map p76, C7

Dark timber, kooky taxidermy and a speakeasy vibe make the Woods a suitable place to hide on those brooding, rainy Melbourne nights. Bunker down for a standout selection of whiskies (including rarer drops), or ditch them altogether for a little Italian subversion: the drinks list includes a string of variations on the classic negroni apéritif. *Cin cin!* (📞03-9521 1900; www.woodsofwindsor.com.au; 108 Chapel St, Windsor; ⏱5.30pm-1am Tue-Sat; 🚌78, 5, 6, 64, 🚊Windsor)

Yellow Bird
BAR

This little bird (see **17** 🍺 Map p76, C7) keeps Windsor's cool kids happy with all-day drinks and diner-style food. It's owned by the drummer from Something for Kate, so the loud, dark rock 'n' roll ambience is genuine, with a passing cast of musos, a fantastic playlist of underground bands and one of the most outrageously kitsch bars in town. (📞03-9533 8983; www.yellowbird.com.au; 122 Chapel St, Windsor; ⏱7.30am-late Mon-Fri, from 8am Sat & Sun; 🚌6, 78, 🚊Windsor)

Railway Hotel
BAR

18 🍺 Map p76, C8

This smart, casual gastropub is divided into numerous design-savvy spaces. The upstairs bar and deck runs one of the area's two gay-oriented Sunday sessions, this one attracting a slightly older, more down-to-earth crowd. Check out the talent (or at least the great skyline view). (📞03-9510 4050; www.therailway.com.au; 29 Chapel St, Windsor; ⏱noon-late; 🚌5, 64, 78, 🚊Windsor)

Borsch, Vodka & Tears
BAR

19 🍺 Map p76, C7

A Chapel St classic, Borsch, Vodka & Tears is a nod to the area's Eastern European influences. The more than 100 vodkas include clear, oak-matured, fruit-infused and traditional *nalewka kresowa* (made according to old Russian and Polish recipes). Staff are clued-up, and the menu includes borscht and blintzes good enough to make your Polish grandpa weep. *Na zdrowie!* (Cheers!) (📞03-9530 2694; www.borschvodkaandtears.com; 173 Chapel St, Windsor; ⏱8am-late Mon-Fri, from 9am Sat & Sun; 🚌6, 78, 🚊Prahran)

Emerson
BAR, CLUB

20 🍺 Map p76, C5

A swanky three-level venue with cocktail bar, club and rooftop bar. On Sunday afternoon the rooftop's a huge hit with gay revellers, who head up to sip skinny bitches (vodka and soda), catch up on the goss and show off all that gym work. (📞03-9825 0900; www.

theemerson.com.au; 143-145 Commercial Rd, South Yarra; ⏰5pm-midnight Thu, noon-5am Fri & Sat, noon-3.30am Sun; 🚊72, 78, 🚉Prahran)

Montereys   BAR

21 🍺 Map p76, C6

This corner bar was inspired by a US road trip, a fact reflected in such cocktails as the Palm Beach Paloma (cucumber, jalapeños, smoky Mezcal, grapefruit, lime) and nosh like lobster rolls (which could use a little more lobster). The real draw, however, is the daily happy hour (5pm to 7pm), with $2 freshly shucked oysters and $6 glasses of bubbles. (☏03-9525 0980; 218 Chapel St, Prahran; ⏰noon-1am Tue-Sat, 11am-11pm Sun; 🛜; 🚊6, 78, 🚉Prahran)

Windsor Castle Hotel   PUB

22 🍺 Map p76, B8

What's not to love about a lime-hued pub with a herd of pink elephants on the roof? The Windsor Castle is a backstreet veteran, full of cosy nooks, sunken pits, fireplaces and flocked wallpaper. Top billing goes to the tiki-themed beer garden, especially fun on hot summer weekend nights. (☏03-9525 0239; www.windsorcastle.com.au; 89 Albert St, Windsor; ⏰3pm-late Mon-Thu, from noon Fri-Sun; 🚊5, 64, 🚉Windsor)

Revolver Upstairs   CLUB

23 🍺 Map p76, C6

Rowdy Revolver can feel like an enormous version of your lounge room, but with 54 hours of nonstop music come the weekend, you're probably glad it's not. Live music, art exhibitions, not to mention interesting local, national and international DJs keep the mixed crowd wide awake. (☏03-9521 5985; www.revolverupstairs.com.au; 229 Chapel St, Prahran; ⏰5pm-4am Tue & Wed, 5pm-6am Thu, 5pm Fri to noon Sat, 24hr 5pm Sat-9am Mon; 🚊6, 78, 🚉Prahran)

Shopping

ArtBoy Gallery   ART

24 🔒 Map p76, C6

ArtBoy displays the talent of up-and-coming and established Melbourne artists. Artworks are affordable, unique and edgy, ranging from stencil to abstract, pop and photography. Even the gallery's rear roller door is a showcase for local creativity, with a feline-themed aerosol portrait by street artist Silly Sully. To see it, head around the corner onto Porter St and then into Brenchley Pl. (☏03-9939 8993; http://artboygallery.com; 99 Greville St, Prahran; ⏰10am-6pm Mon-Thu, to 5pm Sat, 11am-4pm Sun; 🚊6, 72, 78, 🚉Prahran)

Chapel Street Bazaar   VINTAGE

25 🔒 Map p76, C7

Calling this a 'permanent undercover collection of market stalls' won't give you any clue as to what's tucked away here. Bluntly, this old arcade is a sprawling, retro-obsessive riot. Whether it's Italian art glass, modernist furniture, classic Hollywood posters or Noddy eggcups that float your boat, you'll find it here. Warning: prepare to lose all track of time. (📞03-9529 1727; www.facebook.com/ChapelStreetBazaar; 217-223 Chapel St, Prahran; ⏲10am-6pm; 🚊6, 78, 79, 🚋Prahran)

Lunar Store
DESIGN

26 🔒 Map p76, C6

This adorable space belongs to Jules Unwin, who fills it up with her favourite things. It's a great place to score quirky, offbeat design objects by both local and foreign artisans. Snoop around and you might find anything from Danish earthenware pencil holders to Melbourne-made ceramic necklaces and pooch-themed pouches from LA. Fun, contemporary, yet strangely nostalgic. (📞03-9533 7668; www.lunarstore.com.au; 2/127 Greville St, Prahran; ⏲11am-

☑ Top Tip
Artists Lane

Running just behind Chapel St is **Artists Lane** (Artists Lane, Windsor; 🚊5, 6, 64, 78, 🚋Windsor) – Aerosol Alley to south-siders – a long bluestone alley soaked in street art. It's a veritable outdoor gallery, initiated by local artist Wayne Tindall and featuring an ever-evolving canvas of aerosol art, stencils and paste-ups. In the corner of the car park spilling off the laneway, look out for child-like human-animal hybrids – the work of internationally renowned Melbourne artist Kaff-eine.

5pm Mon-Wed, 10am-6pm Thu & Fri, 10am-5pm Sat, 11am-4pm Sun; 🚊6, 72, 78, 🚋Prahran)

Signed & Numbered
ART

27 🔒 Map p76, C6

Art at its democratic best: Signed & Numbered deals in affordable limited-edition prints from more than 60 local and international artists, both emerging and established. Displayed pretty much like vinyl in a record store, the works span numerous print mediums, from etchings, letterpress and lino to screen and digital woodblock. (📞03-9077 6468; http://signedandnumbered.com.au; 153 Greville St, Prahran; ⏲11am-5pm Wed-Fri & Sun, from 10am Sat; 🚊6, 72, 78, 🚋Prahran)

Shelley Panton
HOMEWARES

28 🔒 Map p76, E6

Potter Shelley Panton set up this gorgeous concept store, which stocks her own minimalist tableware alongside other local designers' work and imported goods from around the globe. Give your living space a lift with the likes of bone-china table lamps, mohair throws, graphic-print cotton cushions and whimsical bookends. (📞03-9533 9003; http://shop.shelleypanton.com; 440 Malvern Rd, Prahran; ⏲9am-5.30pm Mon-Sat, from 10am Sun; 🚊72, 🚋Hawksburn)

Greville Records
MUSIC

29 🔒 Map p76, C6

One of the last bastions of the 'old' Greville St, this banging music shop has such a loyal following that the

IVO ANTONIE DE ROOIJ/SHUTTERSTOCK ©

Prahran Market (p81)

great Neil Young invited the owners on stage during a Melbourne concert. The forte here is vinyl, with no shortage of eclectic and limited-edition discs (a super-limited Bob Dylan *Live in Sydney 1966* double vinyl has been discovered here...). (☎03-9510 3012; www.grevillerecords.com.au; 152 Greville St, Prahran; ⏰10am-6pm Mon-Thu & Sat, to 7pm Fri, 11am-5pm Sun; ☒78. 79, ☒Prahran)

Scanlan Theodore
FASHION & ACCESSORIES

30 🛍 Map p76, D4

Scanlan Theodore helped define the Melbourne look in the 1980s and, despite the cut-throat nature of local retail, the label is still going strong with its super-feminine, beautifully tailored everyday and special-occasion wear. Although it's now considered a mature, mainstream label, its creations continue to make a statement, with clean lines and elegant, understated style. (☎03-9824 1800; www.scanlantheodore.com; 566 Chapel St, South Yarra; ⏰10am-6pm Mon-Thu, to 7pm Fri, to 5.30pm Sat, 11am-5pm Sun; ☒78, 79, ☒South Yarra)

Explore

East Melbourne & Richmond

Melbourne is one of the world's great sporting cities, and Richmond and East Melbourne are the absolute nexus for all things sporting. The standout is the mighty Melbourne Cricket Ground. North from here are the genteel streets of East Melbourne, centred on pretty Fitzroy Gardens. On the eastern flank, Richmond is a part-gentrified, part-gritty residential and commercial expanse with interesting eateries.

The Sights in a Day

☀ Start the day along Bridge Rd with breakfast and good coffee at **Touchwood** (p98). Wander up the road afterwards to shop for some discount big-name brands. Explore Richmond's character-filled backstreets to link up with Swan St for more shopping and cafes, and a carnivorous lunch at **Meatmother** (p94).

☀ If you're visiting on the weekend, you may be lucky enough to catch a game of footy or cricket at the **Melbourne Cricket Ground** (p90), otherwise you can visit its hallowed turf on a tour at the National Sports Museum on-site. Across the bridge, sporting buffs can continue their day with a tour of **Melbourne Park** (p98), home to the Australian Tennis Open, or even rent a practice court for a hit.

☾ For an inexpensive Southeast Asian dinner, head to one of the many Vietnamese restaurants on Richmond's Victoria St. Most, including **Thy Thy** (p94), allow you to bring your own (BYO) alcohol, making it a social occasion. Afterwards, catch a gig at the **Corner** (p98) or grab a beer upstairs at its buzzing rooftop bar.

👁 Top Sights

Melbourne Cricket Ground (p90)

💙 Best of Melbourne

Eating
Thy Thy (p94)

Drinking
Mountain Goat Brewery (p98)

Getting There

🚆 **Train** Richmond station is a major interchange for trains on the Alamein, Belgrave, Cranbourne, Frankston, Glen Waverley, Lilydale, Pakenham and Sandringham lines.

🚋 **Tram** Trams run along Victoria St (routes 12 and 109), Bridge Rd (48 and 75), Swan St (70) and Church St (78).

Top Sights
Melbourne Cricket Ground

With a capacity of 100,000 people, the 'G' is one of the world's great sporting venues, hosting cricket in summer and AFL (Australian Football League; Aussie rules) footy in winter. For many Australians it's considered hallowed ground. Make it to a game if you can (highly recommended), but otherwise you can still make your pilgrimage on non-match-day tours that take you through the stands, media and coaches' areas, change rooms and members' lounges. The MCG houses the state-of-the-art National Sports Museum.

👁 Map p92, B3

📞 03-9657 8888

www.mcg.org.au

tour adult/child/family
$23/12/55, incl museum
$32/16/70

🕙 tours 10am-3pm

🚉 Jolimont

AFL Footy Games

Attending a game of AFL footy at a packed MCG is a memorable experience among the atmosphere of 80,000 parochial fans. The game is known for its cracking pace, aerial grabs, long-shot goals, intense physicality and athleticism. The season runs from mid-March to the end of September; tickets are mostly available on match days.

Cricket Matches

Cricket is Victoria's summer love and seeing a test at the 'G' is a must for cricket fans from around the world. The Boxing Day Test is for many sport-mad Melburnians a bigger deal than Christmas itself. Warm days, cricket's leisurely pace and the supporters who've travelled from far and wide often make for spectator theatrics.

National Sports Museum

Hidden away in the bowels of the Melbourne Cricket Ground, this sports museum features exhibits focusing on Australia's favourite sports and historic sporting moments. Kids will love the interactive section where they can test their footy, cricket or netball skills. There's even a hologram of cricketer Shane Warne. Objects on display include the handwritten notes used to define the rules of Australian rules football in 1859 and a collection of baggy green caps worn by a who's who of Aussie cricket (including the legendary Don Bradman).

Ground Tours

On non-match days, go behind the scenes on tours through the stands, media and coaches' areas, into change rooms and out onto the ground.

☑ Top Tips

▶ There are no ground tours on game days.

▶ Discounts are available if you get a combined museum and tour ticket.

▶ If you're in the area and after a taste of a live AFL game, sometimes it's possible to wander in free of charge at three-quarter time (around 1½ hours after starting time) to see the last 30 minutes of the action.

✗ Take a Break

There's no shortage of pubs in the immediate area for a pre-game drink, with the rooftop bar at the Corner (p98) being a top choice.

A bit further along Swan St brings you to a meat-lover's paradise at Meatmother. (p94)

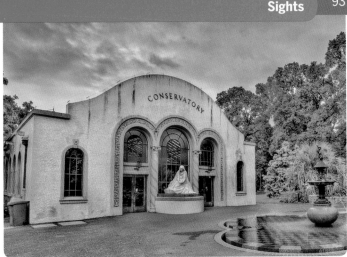

LEONID ANDRONOV/SHUTTERSTOCK ©

Conservatory, Fitzroy Gardens

Sights

Fitzroy Gardens PARK

1 ⊙ Map p92, A2

The city drops away suddenly just east of Spring St, giving way to Melbourne's beautiful backyard, Fitzroy Gardens. The park's stately avenues are lined with English elms, flowerbeds, expansive lawns, strange fountains and a creek. A highlight is **Cooks' Cottage** (adult/child/family $6.50/3.50/18; ⊙9am-5pm), which belonged to the parents of navigator Captain James Cook. The cottage was shipped brick by brick from Yorkshire and reconstructed here in 1934. Nearby is a **visitor centre** (☎03-9658 9658; www.thatsmelbourne.com.au; ⊙9am-5pm) with a cafe attached and the delightful 1930s **Conservatory** (⊙9am-5pm). (www.fitzroygardens.com; Wellington Pde, East Melbourne; ☒Jolimont)

Charles Nodrum Gallery GALLERY

2 ⊙ Map p92, D3

Situated in a lovely old house, this quality commercial gallery specialises in the Australian abstract and alternative art movements from the 1950s to the 1970s. (☎03-9427 0140; www.charlesnodrumgallery.com.au; 267 Church St, Richmond; ⊙11am-6pm Tue-Sat; ☒48, 75, 78)

Scarred Tree
LANDMARK

3 ⊙ Map p92, B3

This fenced-off stump of a river red gum is a rare reminder of pre-colonial Melbourne. The bark was removed by the local Wurundjeri people to fashion into something along the lines of a crib, canoe or shield. (Yarra Park, East Melbourne)

Eating

Minamishima
JAPANESE $$$

4 ✗ Map p92, E3

Hidden down a side street, Minamishima offers possibly the most unique Japanese dining experience this side of the equator. Sit at the bar seats and watch sushi master Koichi Minamishima prepare seafood with surgical precision and serve it one piece at a time. There's only a handful of seats, so book well in advance. (☏03-9429 5180; www.minamishima.com.au; 4 Lord St, Richmond; per person $150; ☺6-10pm Tue-Sat; ☒48, 75)

☑ Top Tip

Cheap Eats

Head upstairs to **Thy Thy** (☏03-9429 1104; 1st fl, 142 Victoria St, Richmond; mains $9-16; ☺9-10pm; ☒North Richmond), a Victoria St original (unchanged since 1987) for cheap and delicious Vietnamese food. No corkage for BYO booze.

Demitri's Feast
GREEK $$

5 ✗ Map p92, D4

This down-to-earth cafe may be tiny, but it's full of huge Greek flavours in dishes such as spanakopita, souvlaki and meze platters. There's an interesting breakfast menu (the zucchini and feta fritters are a standout), and the coffee's excellent too, especially when paired with a traditional Greek sweet. (☏03-9428 8659; www.demitris feast.com.au; 141 Swan St, Richmond; mains $10-24; ☺8am-4pm Tue-Sun; ☒East Richmond)

Meatmother
AMERICAN $$

6 ✗ Map p92, D4

Vegetarians, beware; this eatery is a shrine to the slaughterhouse, as is evident in the meat cleavers hanging on the walls. All meat is smoked over oak, from the 12-hour pulled-pork sandwich to the 20-hour beef brisket. At lunchtime it offers a range of $15 burgers and sandwiches, including a delicious burnt-end bun. Wash it down with some American whiskey. (☏03-9041 5393; www.meatmother.com.au; 167 Swan St, Richmond; mains $20-28; ☺5pm-late Wed & Thu, noon-3pm & 5pm-late Fri-Sun; ☒70)

Richmond Hill Cafe & Larder
CAFE $$

7 ✗ Map p92, C2

Once the domain of well-known cook Stephanie Alexander, this deli-cafe may be looking a little dated, but it's

FILEDIMAGE/SHUTTERSTOCK ©

Cooks' Cottage (p93), Fitzroy Gardens

still excellent. It boasts a top-notch cheese room and a menu ranging from the simple (cheesy toast) to little works of art (bircher muesli with chia-seed cubes and raspberry dust). There are breakfast cocktails for the adventurous. (📞03-9421 2808; www.rhcl. com.au; 48-50 Bridge Rd, Richmond; lunch $12-27; 🕙7am-5pm; 🚊48, 75)

Sabai
THAI $$

8 🍴 Map p92, D4

The traditional wisdom is that Sydney does Thai and Melbourne does Vietnamese, but this little neighbourhood restaurant bucks the trend, serving a delicious mix of classic and modern Thai dishes in smart surrounds. The service is excellent too. (📞03-8528 6884; www.sabairichmond.com.au; 460 Church St, Richmond; mains $17-24; 🕙11.30am-9.30pm Mon-Fri, 4-9.30pm Sat & Sun; 🚊East Richmond)

Baby
ITALIAN $$

9 🍴 Map p92, D4

Arguably the most painfully fashionable spot in Richmond, this bold and buzzy pizzeria has a good vibe and cheery service – and you might spot the odd Aussie TV star. (📞03-9421 4599; www.babypizza.com.au; 631-633 Church St, Richmond; mains $22-35; 🕙7am-11pm; 🚊78)

Understand
Sporting Mad Melbourne

Cynics snicker that sport is the sum of Victoria's culture, although it's hard to hear them above all that cheering, theme-song singing and applause.

Melbourne hosts a disproportionate number of international sporting events, including the Australian Open, Australian Formula One Grand Prix and Melbourne Cup horse race. At the heart of its obsession is Australian Rules Football (AFL, AussieRules or 'the footy'), born in Melbourne in 1858. Today it's followed fanatically, and games regularly attract crowds of 50,000 to 90,000 during the season that runs from March to September. The vast majority of Victorians become obsessed during footy season. They enter tipping competitions at work, discuss hamstring injuries and suspensions over the water cooler, and devour huge chunks of the daily newspapers devoted to mighty victories, devastating losses and the latest bad-boy behaviour (on and off the field).

In early 2017 the inaugural AFL women's league was launched, with traditional rivals Carlton and Collingwood fittingly matched for the showcase game held at Princes Park to a lock-out crowd.

Cricket is Victoria's summer passion and it's the game that truly unites the state with the rest of Australia. It has a stronghold in Victoria, given the hallowed turf of the Melbourne Cricket Ground (MCG) and Cricket Australia's base in Melbourne.

Between footy and cricket seasons, Melburnians choose horse racing as their obsession during the Spring Carnival in October, which culminates with 'the race that stops a nation': the Melbourne Cup, held on the first Tuesday of November. The Cup attracts 120,000 spectators, is watched by 700 million people in more than 170 countries, and most Victorians have the day off as a public holiday.

The 'rectangle' football codes – rugby league (NRL), rugby union and soccer – are also well supported. In the A-League national soccer competition (October to May), Melbourne is represented by two teams, Melbourne Victory and Melbourne City, who both play at the striking honeycomb-roofed AAMI Park. Likewise Melbourne Storm in the National Rugby League (NRL) and the Melbourne Rebels in the Super Rugby (Super 18). International rugby union tests are held yearly in Melbourne at Docklands Stadium.

Corner (p98),

Meatball & Wine Bar   AMERICAN $$

10 Map p92, C4

A branch of a Melbourne chain serving an American take on Italian meatballs. (☑03-9428 3339; www.meatballandwinebar.com.au; 105 Swan St, Richmond; mains $20-22; ☺5pm-late Mon & Tue, noon-late Wed-Sun; ◙70)

Minh Minh   SOUTHEAST ASIAN $

11 Map p92, C1

Minh Minh specialises in fiery Laotian dishes – the herby green-and-red-chilli beef salad is a favourite – but it serves plenty of Vietnamese and Thai staples, too. (☑03-9427 7891; 94 Victoria St, Richmond; mains $7-19; ☺4-10pm Tue, 11.30am-10.30pm Wed-Sun; ◙North Richmond)

Drinking

DT's Hotel   GAY

12 Map p92, D2

This long-standing gay pub hosts drag shows, karaoke, pool competitions and happy hours. (☑03-9428 5724; www.facebook.com/dtspub; 164 Church St, Richmond; ☺6pm-midnight Tue, 4pm-1am Wed-Sat, 2-11pm Sun; ◙78)

○ Local Life
Mountain Goat Brewery
This **local microbrewery** (☎03-9428 1180; www.goatbeer.com.au; 80 North St, Richmond; ⊙5-10pm Wed & Fri; ☒48, 75) occupies a large warehouse in Richmond's backstreets. Sample its range of beers with an $11 tasting paddle while nibbling pizza. There are free brewery tours at 6.30pm on Wednesday. It's tricky to reach: head east on Bridge Rd, then turn left at Burnley St and right at North St.

Public House
BAR

13 🍷 Map p92, D4

Not in any way resembling a public house from any discernible period in history, this swanky bar has been given a striking fit-out using raw and recycled materials. The food's excellent and DJs set up at weekends, attracting a young, good-looking crowd ready to, uh, mingle. (☎03-9421 0187; www.publichouse.com.au; 433-435 Church St, Richmond; ⊙noon-late Tue-Sun; ☒East Richmond)

Slowbeer
CRAFT BEER

14 🍷 Map p92, E3

The walls of this little shop are lined with craft beer for sale, but you can pull up a seat at the central wooden table and settle in for a drink and a snack. (☎03-9421 3838; www.slowbeer.com.au; 468 Bridge Rd, Richmond; ⊙2-8pm Mon-Wed, noon-9pm Thu-Sat, noon-8pm Sun; ☒48, 75)

Touchwood
CAFE

15 🍷 Map p92, E3

There's plenty of space both indoors and in the courtyard of this light, airy cafe housed in a former recycled-furniture store (hence the name). The coffee's single origin and the doughnuts at the counter are difficult to resist. (☎03-9429 9347; www.touchwoodcafe.com; 480 Bridge Rd, Richmond; ⊙7am-4pm; ☒48, 75)

Entertainment

Corner
LIVE MUSIC

16 ⭐ Map p92, C4

The band room here is one of Melbourne's most popular midsize venues, and it's seen plenty of loud and live action over the years, from Dinosaur Jr to the Buzzcocks. If your ears need a break, there's a friendly front bar. The rooftop has city views but gets packed, and often with a different crowd from the music fans below. (☎03-9427 7300; www.cornerhotel.com; 57 Swan St, Richmond; ⊙4pm-late Mon-Fri, noon-3am Sat, noon-1am Sun; ☒Richmond)

Melbourne Park
SPECTATOR SPORT

17 ⭐ Map p92, A3

Home to the **Australian Open tennis championship** (www.australianopen.com; ⊙Jan), the Melbourne Park precinct has 34 courts, including its centrepiece, **Rod Laver Arena** (☎03-9286

LEONARD ZHUKOVSKY/SHUTTERSTOCK ©

Rod Laver Arena

1600; www.rodlaverarena.com.au; 🚋70), and **Hisense Arena** (www.hisensearena.com.au), which also hosts netball and basketball teams. (☎03-9286 1600; www.mopt.com.au; Olympic Blvd, Melbourne; 🚋70)

Shopping

Pookipoiga   GIFTS & SOUVENIRS

18 🔒 Map p92, C2

Everything is ethically produced, sustainable and animal friendly at this cute little gift store, packed with interesting things. There's a great selection of quirky greeting cards, loud socks, toiletries and scarves. (☎03-8589 4317; www.pookipoiga.com; 64 Bridge Rd, Richmond; ⏱9.30am-5pm; 🚋48, 75)

Lily & the Weasel   GIFTS & SOUVENIRS

19 🔒 Map p92, D4

A mix of beautiful things from around the globe is stocked at this interesting store, alongside the work of local designers (such as children's toys and scarves), toiletries and Robert Gordon ceramics. (☎03-9421 1008; www.lily-andtheweasel.com.au; 173 Swan St, Richmond; ⏱11am-5pm Tue-Sun; 🚋70)

Local Life
East Brunswick

Getting There

🚋 1, 19

🚆 Brunswick

Brunswick and East Brunswick are easily accessed 20 minutes from the city.

Multicultural Brunswick is a wonderful mix of Middle Eastern, Greek, African and Indian immigrants, who converge on Sydney Rd to create a lively strip with some fantastic eating. More recent times has seen an influx of the younger hip crowd who've added another layer of vibrancy, particularly in East Brunswick, which has some of Melbourne's coolest bars and cafes along Lygon St.

1 Brunch at Pope Joan

Pope Joan (📞03-9388 8858; www.pope
joan.com.au; 75-79 Nicholson St, East Brunswick; mains $15; ⏰7.30am-3pm; 🚻; 🚌96)
has a menu of creative comfort food,
strong coffee and 'liquid breakfasts' of
Bloody Marys and spritzers.

2 Sustainable Stopover

Ceres (📞03-9389 0100; www.ceres.org.au;
cnr Roberts & Stewart Sts, East Brunswick;
admission free; ⏰9am-5pm, cafe 9am-3pm
Mon-Fri, to 4pm Sat & Sun; 🚌96) is a two-
decades-old community environment
built on a former rubbish tip. Take a
stroll around the permaculture and
bushfood nursery, community market
and the great bookstore.

3 Get Caffeinated

A big player in Melbourne's coffee movement, this East Brunswick
warehouse-style cafe is the original
roaster for **Padre Coffee** (📞03-9381
1881; www.padrecoffee.com.au; 438 Lygon St,
East Brunswick; ⏰7am-2pm Mon, to 4pm Tue-
Sat, 8am-4pm Sun; 🚻; 🚌1, 6) and brews
its premium single-origins and blends.

4 Something Sweet

Sugardough (📞03-9380 4060; www.
sugardough.com.au; 163 Lygon St, East
Brunswick; meals from $8.80; ⏰7.30am-
5pm Tue-Fri, to 4pm Sat, 8am-4pm Sun;
🚻; 🚌1, 6) does a roaring trade in
homemade pies (including vegetarian
ones), panini, homebaked bread and
pastries. Mismatched cutlery and cups
and saucers make it rather like being
at Grandma's on family-reunion day.

5 Pre-dinner Drink

A classic East Brunswick local, the
Alderman (📞03-9380 9003; 134 Lygon St,
East Brunswick; ⏰5-11pm Tue-Thu, to 1am Fri,
3pm-1am Sat, 3-11pm Sun; 🚻; 🚌1, 6) has
an inviting traditional heavy wooden
bar, an open fireplace, a good beer
and cocktail selection, and welcoming
staff. There's a small courtyard and
you can order from restaurant Bar
Idda next door.

6 Dinner at Rumi

Rumi (📞03-9388 8255; www.rumirestaurant.
com.au; 116 Lygon St, East Brunswick; dishes
$13-28; ⏰6-10pm; 🚌1, 6) serves tradition-
al Lebanese cooking and contemporary
interpretations of old Persian dishes.
The *sigara boregi* (cheese and pinenut
pastries) are a local institution, and
tasty mains are balanced with an interesting selection of vegetable dishes.

7 Craft Beer Time

Alehouse Project (📞03-9387 1218; www.
thealehouseproject.com.au; 98-100 Lygon St,
East Brunswick; ⏰3pm-late Mon-Fri, noon-
late Sat & Sun; 🚻; 🚌1, 6) is where beer
lovers convene and compare notes
on the 12 craft beers on tap. Beer-hall
style seating and a courtyard.

8 Live Music

The **Retreat** (📞03-9380 4090; www.
retreathotelbrunswick.com.au; 280 Sydney Rd,
Brunswick; ⏰noon-1am Mon-Thu & Sun, to 3am
Fri & Sat; 🚌19, 🚆Brunswick) is a beloved
venue, a 15-minute walk or short cab
ride away on Sydney Rd. Find your hab-
itat – garden backyard, grungy band
room or intimate front bar – and relax.

Explore

Fitzroy & Collingwood

A short tram ride from the city centre delivers you to the doorstep of some of the hippest enclaves in Melbourne, where up-to-the-minute eateries and mid-century furniture stores sit comfortably next to decades-old pubs and live-music venues. Fitzroy and Collingwood have long had a reputation for vice and squalor and, despite ongoing gentrification, there's still enough grit holding these areas in check.

The Sights in a Day

☀️ Start in the warehouse-filled backstreets of Collingwood, with an single-sourced coffee at **Proud Mary** (p112) before heading around the corner to check out their roastery. Then seek out Melbourne's urban and contemporary art scene at **Gertrude Contemporary** (p107) and **Backwoods Gallery** (p108).

☼ Venture down Smith St for lunch, and choose from hot spots such as **Huxtaburger** (p110) for brioche-bun burgers or go upmarket at **Ides** (p109). **Gelato Messina** (p108) is a must for a post-lunch sugar hit. Head around the corner to Gertrude St for some of Melbourne's best boutique stores including **Third Drawer Down** (p116), **Aesop** (p116) and **Obüs** (p117). Push onwards to Fitzroy's Brunswick St and stock up on vinyl at **Polyester Records** (p116) before lining up for delectable pastries at **Lune Croissanterie** (p108).

🌙 Still on Brunswick St, drop in for an award-winning cocktail at **Black Pearl** (p112) then head to **Naked for Satan's** (p112) rooftop bar for sensational views and pre-dinner drinks and tapas. Head back to Gertrude St for your reservation at **Cutler & Co** (p108), followed by drinks at **Marion** (p112) or **Everleigh.** (p112) End the night with a gig at **The Tote** (p114) or **Gasometer** (p114).

For a local's night out in Fitzroy and Collingwood, see p104.

🔍 **Local Life**

Fitzroy & Collingwood Pub Crawl

💗 **Best of Melbourne**

Eating

Proud Mary (p112)

Smith & Deli (p108)

Cutler & Co (p108)

Charcoal Lane (p109)

Gelato Messina (p108)

Lune Croissanterie (p108)

Drinking

Naked for Satan (p112)

Stomping Ground Brewery & Beer Hall (p113)

Everleigh (p112)

Black Pearl (p112)

Getting There

🚊 **Tram** Fitzroy and Collingwood are a short tram ride from the city centre. Tram 11 runs along Brunswick St and tram 86 along Smith St.

🚆 **Train** Collingwood station is located just near Hoddle St and is a short walk to Smith St. The station is served by the Hurstbridge line.

Local Life
Fitzroy & Collingwood Pub Crawl

All of the following pubs are Fitzroy and Collingwood local classics. Expect a welcoming laid-back crowd, rather than your 'too cool for school' crew. All have pub meals available for a pre-drink feed; highly advisable for fueling up on this pub crawl.

❶ **Builders Arms Hotel**
A completely re-imagined bad old boozer, the **Builders Arms** (📞03-9417 7700; www.buildersarmshotel.com. au/bar-bistro; 211 Gertrude St, Fitzroy; ⊘noon-late; 🚌86) has retained its charm despite theatrical new threads. Come for a pot by all means, but there's also decent wine by the glass and counter meals.

❷ **Grace Darling**
Grace Darling (📞03-9416 0055; www.thegracedarling hotel.com.au; 114 Smith St, Collingwood; mains $18-30; ⊘noon-1am Mon-Sat, to 11pm

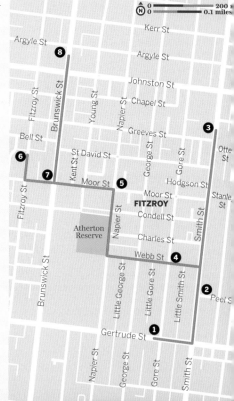

Sun; 🚍86) has been given a bit of spit and polish by some well-known Melbourne foodies, and while the chicken parma remains, it is certainly not how you know it (more a terracotta bake of chargrilled chook, ham, slow-roasted tomato and parmesan). There's also live music, mainly aimed at the young indie crowd.

❸ Feeling Peckish?

There are plenty of souvlaki and kebab joints open till early morning, but **Po' Boy Quarter** (☑03-9419 2130; www. poboyquarter.com.au; 295 Smith St, Fitzroy; rolls $12-15; ⏰11.30am-11pm Sun-Wed, to 1am Thu-Sat; 🚍86), the boys behind the Gumbo Kitchen truck, have parked permanently on Smith St with this smart canteen-style eatery. Wolf down a roll of pulled pork, shrimp with Louisiana hot sauce or fried green tomatoes with Cajun slaw.

❹ Union Club Hotel

A die-hard local, the **Union Club Hotel** (☑03-9417 2926; www.unionclubhotel.com. au; 164 Gore St, Fitzroy; ⏰3pm-late Mon-Wed, noon-late Thu-Sat, noon-11pm Sun; 🚍86) is swimming in earthy good vibes, and happy chatter from the relaxed indie crowd. The large curved bar is one of Melbourne's best spots to park yourself, the food is honest pub nosh, and the beer garden and rooftop decking make for perfect lazing on a hot day.

❺ Napier Hotel

The **Napier** (☑03-9419 4240; www. thenapierhotel.com; 210 Napier St, Fitzroy;

⏰3-11pm Mon-Thu, noon-1am Fri, noon-11pm Sat, 1-11pm Sun; 🚍86, 11) has stood on this corner for over a century; many beers have been pulled as the face of the neighbourhood changed. Worm your way around the central bar to the boisterous dining room for an iconic Bogan Burger. Head upstairs to check out the gallery, too.

❻ The Standard

Flaunting a great beer garden, the **Standard** (☑03-9419 4793; 293 Fitzroy St, Fitzroy; ⏰3-10pm Mon, to 11pm Tue, noon-11pm Wed-Sat, noon-10pm Sun; 🚍96, 11) is anything but its moniker. The backstreet local has down-to-earth bar staff, a truly eclectic crowd and an atmosphere defined by live music, footy on-screen, and loud and enthusiastic chatter.

❼ Labour in Vain

Boy's own beer barn, the **Labour in Vain** (☑03-9417 5955; www.labourinvain. com.au; 197a Brunswick St, Fitzroy; ⏰3pm-late Mon-Wed, 2pm-late Thu-Sat, 2-11pm Sun; 🚍11) has a pool table and lots of dingy period charm. Upstairs there's a deck perfect for lazy afternoons doing a spot of Brunswick St people-watching.

❽ Bar Open

This long-established **bar** (☑03-9415 9601; www.baropen.com.au; 317 Brunswick St, Fitzroy; ⏰3pm-3am; 🚍11) is often open when everything else is closed, despite the name suggests. The bar attracts a relaxed, young local crowd and bands play in the upstairs loft most nights and are almost always free.

Alexandra Pde (Eastern Hwy)

To Northcote (3km)

FITZROY

COLLINGWOOD

Atherton Reserve

Gertrude Contemporary Art Space

Alcaston Gallery

Victoria Pde

0   400 m
0   0.25 miles

Union Club Hotel (p104)

Sights

Alcaston Gallery
GALLERY

1 ⦿ Map p106, A5

Set in an imposing boom-style terrace, the Alcaston showcases international and Australian art, with a focus on the work of living Indigenous Australian artists. The gallery works directly with Indigenous communities and is particularly attentive to cultural sensitivities; it shows a wide range of styles from traditional to contemporary. Check the website for exhibitions. (☏03-9418 6444; www.alcastongallery.com.au; 11 Brunswick St, Fitzroy; admission free; ☺10am-6pm Tue-Fri, 11am-5pm Sat; 🚊11)

Gertrude Contemporary Art Space
GALLERY

2 ⦿ Map p106, B5

This nonprofit gallery and studio complex has been going strong for nearly 30 years; many of its alumni are now certified famous artists. The monthly exhibition openings often see crowds spilling out onto the street. The gallery will be relocating in mid-2017, and its new venue is yet to be confirmed. Also check out its new space nearby, **Glasshouse** (www.gertrude.org.au; 44 Glasshouse Rd, Collingwood; ☺noon-5pm Tue-Sat; 🚊109, 86). (☏03-9419 3406; www.gertrude.org.au; 200 Gertrude St, Fitzroy; ☺11am-5.30pm Tue-Fri, to 4.30pm Sat; 🚊86)

Local Life
Fitzroy Swimming Pool
Between laps, locals love catching a few rays up in the bleachers or on the lawn at this **local favourite** (📞03-9205 5180; 160 Alexandra Pde, Fitzroy; adult/child/under 5yr $6.50/3.30/free; ⏰6am-9pm Mon-Thu, to 8pm Fri, 8am-6pm Sat & Sun; 🚊11); there's also a toddler pool.

Backwoods Gallery

GALLERY

3 ◉ Map p106, D2

Set up in 2010 by a team of Melbourne street artists, the Backwoods Gallery promotes and exhibits works by Australian and international artists, with a focus on urban contemporary art, stencil, street art and illustration in its warehouse space in a Collingwood backstreet. (📞03-9041 3606; www.backwoods.gallery; 25 Easey St, Collingwood; ⏰noon-6pm Tue-Sun; 🚊86)

Eating

Cutler & Co

MODERN AUSTRALIAN $$$

4 🍴 Map p106, A4

Hyped for all the right reasons, this restaurant and its attentive, informed staff and joy-inducing dishes have quickly made it one of Melbourne's top places for fine dining. The menu strives to incorporate the best seasonal produce across the à la carte offering, the degustation menu (from $150), and the casual Sunday lunch designed for sharing. (📞03-9419 4888; www.cutlerandco.com.au; 55 Gertrude St, Fitzroy; mains $36-48; ⏰6pm-late Tue-Sun, lunch from noon Sun; 🚊86)

Gelato Messina

GELATO $

5 🍴 Map p106, C3

Messina is hyped as Melbourne's best ice-creamery and its popularity is evident in the queues of people in summer waiting to wrap their smackers around such smooth flavours as salted coconut and mango, poached figs in marsala, or blood-orange sorbet. You can watch the ice-cream makers at work through glass windows inside. (www.gelatomessina.com; 237 Smith St, Fitzroy; 1 scoop $4.80; ⏰noon-11pm Sun-Thu, to 11.30pm Fri & Sat; 🚊86)

Lune Croissanterie

BAKERY $

6 🍴 Map p106, B1

The queues may have you turning on your heel, but good things come to those who wait, and here they come in the form of some of the best pastries you'll ever taste – from the lemon-curd cruffin to a classic almond croissant. In the centre of this warehouse space sits a climate-controlled glass cube, the Lune Lab, where the magic happens. (www.lunecroissanterie.com; 119 Rose St, Fitzroy; pastries $5.50-12.50; ⏰7.30am-3pm Mon, Thu & Fri, from 8am Sat & Sun; 🚊11)

Smith & Deli

DELI, VEGAN $

7 🍴 Map p106, B3

Full of '50s-NYC-deli charm with a vegan twist, this little takeaway creates what might be the closest vegetarians will get to eating meat – it's even been known to fool a few carnivores. Sandwiches are made to order and filled with all the favourites; try the Rubenstein, loaded with 'pastrami', sauerkraut and pickles, or opt for the Club Sandwiches Not Seals. (☏03-9042 4117; www.smithanddaughters.com; 111 Moor St, Fitzroy; sandwiches $10-15; ⏱8am-6pm Tue-Sat; ✈; 🚊11)

Charcoal Lane   MODERN AUSTRALIAN $$

8 🍴 Map p106, B5

Housed in an old bluestone former bank, this training restaurant for Indigenous and disadvantaged young people is one of the best places to try native flora and fauna; menu items may include pan-seared emu fillet with lemon-myrtle risotto and wattleseed crème brûlée. The chef's native tasting plate for two ($30) is a great place to start. Weekend bookings advised. (☏03-9418 3400; www.charcoal-lane.com.au; 136 Gertrude St, Fitzroy; mains $19-31; ⏱noon-3pm & 6-9pm Tue-Sat; 🚊86)

Easey's   BURGERS $$

9 🍴 Map p106, D2

Biting into burgers and gulping back beers in a graffiti-covered old train carriage perched on top of a backstreet rooftop – it doesn't get much more Collingwood than this. Easey's does a handful of no-holds-barred burgers that will have your cholesterol rising faster than you can say 'gimme the side of triple-fried dim

sims'. (http://easeys.com.au; 48 Easey St, Collingwood; burgers $10-23; ⏱11am-10pm Sun-Thu, to 11pm Fri & Sat; 🚊86)

Horn   AFRICAN $$

10 🍴 Map p106, D2

Straight outta Addis Ababa, the flavours and feel of this Ethiopian restaurant are as authentic as its homemade *injera* (soft bread; prepared fresh daily). Tear it into your meal using your fingers and wash it down with Ethiopian beer. There's jazz on Thursday evening, and on Sunday traditional Ethiopian music with a modern take. (☏03-9417 4670; www.thehorncafe.com.au; 20 Johnston St, Collingwood; mains $16-21; ⏱6pm-late Wed-Sat, 3-10pm Sun; 🚊86)

Ides   MODERN AUSTRALIAN $$$

11 🍴 Map p106, C5

What started as a pop-up is now a permanent restaurant. Word spread quickly that Attica (p144) sous chef Peter Gunn had started his own establishment, where he does the term 'creative' justice with a contemporary take on fine dining. It's a six-course, seasonal affair preceded by hot bread with dangerously good house peanut butter. (☏03-9939 9542; www.idesmelbourne.com.au; 92 Smith St, Collingwood; 6-course degustation $110; ⏱from 6pm Wed-Sun; 🚊86)

Saint Crispin   MODERN AUSTRALIAN $$$

12 🍴 Map p106, C3

The stylish interiors, light-filled space, prompt service and excellent food make this one of the best places for fine dining in the inner city. You can choose from two or three courses, or opt for the chef's tasting menu (from $100). The duo behind the restaurant spent time working together at Michelin-starred The Square in London. (☎03-9419 2202; www.saintcrispin. com.au; 300 Smith St, Collingwood; 2/3 courses $50/65; ☺6pm-late Tue-Thu, noon-late Fri-Sun; ☒86)

Belle's Hot Chicken AMERICAN $$

14 ✖ Map p106, B5

Chef Morgan McGlone knew he was onto a good thing while honing his kitchen skills in the States. But ever since he brought Nashville fried chicken back to Australia and paired it with natural wine, it's been a finger-lickin' revolution. Launch into tenders, drumsticks or wings with your preference of heat (note: 'Really F**kin Hot' is so named for good reason). (☎03-9077 0788; http://belleshotchicken.com; 150 Gertrude St, Fitzroy; chicken & a side from $17; ☺noon-10pm Sun-Thu, to 11pm Fri & Sat; ☒86)

✔️ Top Tip

Northcote & Thornbury

If you enjoy Fitzroy and Collingwood's vibe, stay on tram 86 for a short ride up High St to Northcote and Thornbury for more band venues, cool cafes and great restaurants.

Hotel Jesus MEXICAN $$

14 ✖ Map p106, C4

Set in an old post-office building, this brash retro cantina is going for fun, with gleaming tiles, red folding chairs and a daggy picture menu. Street food is the focus, particularly tostadas, topped with flavours that are a bit hit-and-miss, sadly. (www.hoteljesus.com. au; 174 Smith St, Collingwood; dishes $6-16; ☺noon-late Wed-Sun, Taco Wey shop noon-5pm Tue, to 6pm Wed-Sat; ☒86)

Huxtaburger BURGERS $

15 ✖ Map p106, C4

This American-style burger joint is a hit for its crinkle-cut chips in old-school containers (go the spicy chipotle salt), tasty burgers (veg options available) on glazed brioche buns, and bottled craft beers. Other branches are in the **city** (Fulham Pl; burgers $7-14; ☺11.30am-10pm; ☒Flinders St) and **Prahran** (203 High St, Prahran; burgers from $10; ☺11.30am-10pm Sun-Thu, to 11pm Fri & Sat; ☒6, 78, ☒Prahran). (☎03-9417 6328; www.huxtaburger.com.au; 106 Smith St, Collingwood; burgers $10-14.50; ☺11.30am-10pm Sun-Thu, to 11pm Fri & Sat; ☒86)

Project Forty Nine CAFE, DELI $$

16 ✖ Map p106, D4

Project Forty Nine brings a slice of the country to Collingwood's industrial backstreets with this outpost of its original cafe in Beechworth, regional Victoria. The huge, airy warehouse incorporates deli, cafe, restaurant and wine bar, focusing on a fusion of

Napier Hotel (p105)

country Victorian produce and Italian flavours in the cafe and restaurant, while the wine bar showcases north-eastern Victorian wines. (☏03-9419 4449; www.projectfortynine.com.au; 107 Cambridge St, Collingwood; cafe mains $13-16, restaurant mains $26-31; ⊙cafe 7am-4pm, deli 9am-6pm Wed-Mon; 🚋86)

Smith Street Alimentari

CAFE, DELI **$$**

17 ✕ Map p106, C3

A winning Italian deli-cafe combo offering take-home meals, panini, salads, fresh pasta and rotisserie meats. The expansive space extends to a dining area with a Mediterranean-inspired menu and lovely rear courtyard. (☏03-9416 1666; www.alimentari.com.au/smith-street; 302 Smith St, Collingwood; panini $9.50-11.50, mains $10-24; ⊙8am-6pm Mon-Wed & Sat, to 7pm Thu & Fri; 🛜; 🚋86)

Vegie Bar

VEGETARIAN **$$**

18 ✕ Map p106, B1

An oldie but a goodie, this cavernous warehouse eatery has been feeding droves of Melbourne's veggie-loving residents for over 20 years. Expect inventive fare and big servings from its menu of delicious thin-crust pizzas, tasty salads, burgers and curries, as well as great smoothies and fresh juices. Also has a fascinating selection of raw food dishes, and plenty of

vegan choices. (☏03-9417 6935; www.
vegiebar.com.au; 380 Brunswick St, Fitzroy;
mains $13-18; ☺11am-10pm Sun-Thu, to
10.30pm Fri & Sat; 🛜🖊; 🚌11)

Drinking

Black Pearl
COCKTAIL BAR

19 🚇 Map p106, B2

After 15 years in the game, Black
Pearl goes from strength to strength,
winning awards and receiving global
accolades along the way. Low lighting,
leather banquettes and candles set the
mood downstairs. Prop at the bar to
study the extensive cocktail list or let
the expert bartenders concoct something to your taste. Upstairs is the
table-service Attic Bar; book ahead.
(☏03-9417 0455; www.blackpearlbar.com.au;
304 Brunswick St, Fitzroy; ☺5pm-3am, Attic
Bar 7pm-2am Thu-Sat; 🚌11)

Marion
WINE BAR

20 🚇 Map p106, A4

Melbourne's poster-boy chef, Andrew
McConnell, knew what he was doing
when he opened Marion. The wine
list is one of the area's most impressive and the space – catering to both
stop-ins and long, romantic chats – is
a pleasure to be in. Food changes
regularly, but expect charcuterie from
McConnell's butcher Meatsmith and
specials with a European bent (dishes
$10 to $34). (☏03-9419 6262; www.
marionwine.com.au; 53 Gertrude St, Fitzroy;
☺5-11pm Mon-Thu, noon-11pm Fri, 8am-11pm
Sat & Sun; 🚌86)

Everleigh
COCKTAIL BAR

Sophistication and bartending
standards are off the charts at this
upstairs hidden nook (see **13** ✖ Map
p106, B5). Settle into a leather booth in
the intimate setting with a few friends
for conversation, and exclaiming
over classic 'golden era' cocktails like
you've never tasted before. (www.theev-
erleigh.com; 150-156 Gertrude St, Fitzroy;
☺5.30pm-1am; 🚌86)

Naked for Satan
BAR

21 🚇 Map p106, B2

Vibrant, loud and reviving an appar-
ent Brunswick St legend (a man nick-
named Satan who would get down
and dirty, naked because of the heat,
in an illegal vodka distillery under the
shop), this place packs a punch with
its popular *pintxos* (Basque tapas; $1
to $2), huge range of beverages, and
unbeatable roof terrace (Naked in the
Sky) with wraparound balcony. (☏03-
9416 2238; www.nakedforsatan.com.au; 285
Brunswick St, Fitzroy; ☺noon-midnight Sun-
Thu, to 1am Fri & Sat; 🚌11)

Proud Mary
CAFE

22 🚇 Map p106, D3

A champion for direct-trade, single-
origin coffee, this quintessential
industrial Collingwood red-brick
space takes its caffeine seriously. It's
consistently packed, not only for the
excellent brew but also for the equally
top-notch food, such as ricotta hotcakes or free-range pork with fennel

crackling. (☎03-9417 5930; 172 Oxford St, Collingwood; ⏰7.30am-4pm Mon-Fri, 8.30am-4pm Sat & Sun; 🛜; 🚌86)

Bar Liberty
BAR

23 🚇 Map p106, C2

From a team of hospitality heavy-weights, Bar Liberty is bringing care-fully selected wines (over 300 on the list) and expertly crafted cocktails to Fitzroy minus any pretentiousness. The approach is laid-back, the atmosphere is relaxed and the dining focus is on bold, refined food. There are monthly wine dinners upstairs and a rear court-yard beer garden, Drinkwell. (http://barliberty.com; 234 Johnston St, Fitzroy; ⏰5pm-late Mon-Sat & from noon Sun; 🚌86)

Industry Beans
CAFE

24 🚇 Map p106, A2

It's all about coffee chemistry at this warehouse cafe tucked in a Fitzroy side street. The coffee guide takes you through the speciality styles on offer (roasted on-site), from AeroPress and pourover to cold drip and espresso, and helpful staff take the pressure off decid-ing. The food menu (brunch $12 to $35) is ambitious but doesn't always hit the mark. (☎03-9417 1034; www.industrybeans.com; 3/62 Rose St, Fitzroy; ⏰7am-4pm Mon-Fri, 8am-4pm Sat & Sun; 🛜; 🚌96, 11)

Sircuit
GAY

25 🚇 Map p106, C5

Hugely popular with a big cross section of gay men, Sircuit is an old-

school gay bar with pool tables, drag shows, a back room and, as the night progresses, a heaving dance floor. (www.sircuit.com.au; 103 Smith St, Fitzroy; ⏰7.30pm-late Wed-Sun; 🚌86)

Stomping Ground Brewery & Beer Hall
BREWERY

26 🚇 Map p106, D4

This inviting brewery set in a former textile factory is a relaxed, leafy retreat with exposed-brick walls, hanging plants, a kids' play area and a large central bar. There are 15 to 25 Stomping Ground beers on tap, as well as rotating guest beers, and a menu of wood-fired pizzas, burgers and salads. (☎03-9415 1944; www.stompingground.beer; 100 Gipps St, Collingwood; ⏰11.30am-11pm Mon-Thu, to 1am Fri & Sat; 🛜🚻; 🚌109, 🚉Collingwood)

Laird
GAY, PUB

27 🚇 Map p106, D4

This long-running men-only pub comes with lots of leather, beer and brawn. Who's yer daddy? And you don't have to worry about getting home: there's accommodation on-site (from $120). There's a calendar of events; check the website for details. (☎03-9417 2832; www.lairdhotel.com; 149 Gipps St, Abbotsford; ⏰5pm-late Mon-Sat, from 4pm Sun; 🚉Collingwood)

Noble Experiment BAR

28 🚇 Map p106, C3

If 1920s Prohibition-era cocktails are your tipple, then swing by the Noble Experiment for a bottle-aged negroni, a bootleggers iced tea or a Kentucky cobbler. Spread over three levels, the decor hints at New York old-world charm and there's a seriously good food offering, from a chef's menu to slow-cooked meats designed for sharing. (☎03-9416 0058; www.thenobleexperiment.com.au; 284 Smith St, Collingwood; ⏱5pm-late Wed & Thu, noon-late Fri-Sun; 🚌86)

Panama Dining Room & Bar BAR

29 🚇 Map p106, C3

Disappear up the stairs to where Smith St's traded in for a Manhattan feel at this warehouse space with huge arched windows. Sip serious cocktails, such as a barrel-aged negroni or a pineapple-and-chipotle daiquiri, while snacking on BBQ king prawns or grilled saganaki. For a more serious feed,

Top Tip

Keith Haring Mural

Anyone with an interest in street art will want to check out the **Keith Haring mural** (Smith St, Collingwood; 🚌86), painted by the late New York artist on his visit in 1984. It adorns the side of the former Collingwood Technical School, next door to The Tote on Johnston St.

park yourself in the dining area for the Euro-inspired menu with an Australian twist. (☎03-9417 7663; www.thepanama.com.au; 3rd fl, 231 Smith St, Fitzroy; ⏱bar 5pm-late, restaurant from 6pm; 🚌86)

Peel Hotel GAY, CLUB

30 🚇 Map p106, D4

The Peel is one of the best-known and most popular gay venues in Melbourne. It's the last stop of a big night. (☎03-9419 4762; www.thepeel.com.au; 113 Wellington St, Collingwood; ⏱11pm-5am Thu, to 7am Fri & Sat; 🚌86)

Entertainment

The Tote LIVE MUSIC

31 ⭐ Map p106, D3

One of Melbourne's most iconic live-music venues, this divey Collingwood pub has a great roster of local and international punk and hardcore bands, and one of the best jukeboxes in the universe. Its temporary closure in 2010 brought Melbourne to a stop, literally: people protested on city-centre streets against the liquor-licensing laws that were blamed for the closure. (☎03-9419 5320; www.thetotehotel.com; cnr Johnston & Wellington Sts, Collingwood; ⏱4pm-late Wed-Sun; 🚌86)

Gasometer LIVE MUSIC

32 ⭐ Map p106, D1

This corner bluestone pub features a cosy front bar, an excellent line-up of bands most nights – from up-and-coming local acts to punk and indie

MICHAEL COYNE/GETTY IMAGES ©

Shopping on Brunswick St (p116)

big names – and one of the best band rooms in the city, with a mezzanine level and a retractable roof for open-air gigs. (☎03-9416 3335; www.thegasometerhotel.com.au; 484 Smith St, Collingwood; ⏰4pm-midnight Tue & Wed, 4pm-2am Thu, noon-3am Fri & Sat, noon-midnight Sun; 🚊86)

Night Cat
LIVE MUSIC

33 ⭐ Map p106, B2

The Night Cat is a barn-sized space with a dance floor that sees lots of action. Music is generally in the Latin, jazz or funk vein. Offers salsa dance classes ($20) on Sunday night. (☎03-9417 0090; www.thenightcat.com.au; 141 Johnston St, Fitzroy; ⏰9pm-3am Fri & Sat, 7pm-3am Sun; 🚊11)

Workers Club
LIVE MUSIC

34 ⭐ Map p106, A4

The Workers Club pulls in some decent live gigs in the band room most nights, while the front bar and beer garden pack out with punters knocking back beer and cocktail jugs and fuelling up on comfort pub grub. (☎03-9415 6558; www.theworkersclub.com.au; cnr Brunswick & Gertrude Sts, Fitzroy; ⏰4pm-1am Mon-Wed, noon-1am Thu-Sun; 🚊86, 11)

Shopping

Third Drawer Down
HOMEWARES

35 🔒 Map p106, B4

It all started with its signature tea-towel designs (now found in MoMA in New York) at this 'museum of art souvenirs'. It makes life beautifully unusual by stocking absurdist pieces with a sense of humour as well as high-end art by well-known designers. Giant watermelon stools sit next to Yayoi Kusama's ceramic plates and scarves by Ai Weiwei. (www.thirddrawerdown.com; 93 George St, Fitzroy; ⏰10am-6pm; 🚃86)

Mud Australia
CERAMICS

36 🔒 Map p106, B5

You'll find some of the most aesthetically beautiful – as well as functional – porcelainware at Australian-designed Mud. Coffee mugs, milk pourers, salad bowls and serving plates come in muted pastel colours with a raw matte finish. (☎03-9419 5161; www.mudaustralia.com; 181 Gertrude St, Fitzroy; ⏰10am-6pm Mon-Fri, to 5pm Sat, noon-5pm Sun; 🚃86)

Polyester Records
MUSIC

37 🔒 Map p106, B1

This popular record store has been selling Melburnians independent music from around the world for decades, and it also has a great range of local stuff. The knowledgeable staff will help you find what you're looking for and can offer great suggestions. (☎03-9419 5137; www.polyesterrecords.com; 387 Brunswick St, Fitzroy; ⏰10am-8pm Mon-Thu & Sat, to 9pm Fri, 11am-6pm Sun; 🚃11)

Aesop
COSMETICS

38 🔒 Map p106, C5

This homegrown empire specialises in citrus- and botanical-based aromatic balms, hair masques, scents, cleansers and oils in simple packaging for both men and women. There are plenty of branches around town (and plenty of opportunities to sample the products in many of Melbourne's cafe bathrooms). (☎03-9419 8356; www.aesop.com; 242 Gertrude St, Fitzroy; ⏰11am-5pm Sun & Mon, 10am-6pm Tue-Fri, 10am-5pm Sat; 🚃86)

Local Life

Rose Street Artists' Market

One of Melbourne's most popular **art-and-craft markets** (www.rosestmarket.com.au; 60 Rose St, Fitzroy; ⏰11am-5pm Sat & Sun; 🚃11) showcases the best of local designers. Here you'll find up to 70 stalls selling matte silver jewellery, clothing, ceramics and iconic Melbourne screen prints. After shopping, head to the attached Young Blood's Diner (7am to 5pm Wednesday to Sunday) for rooftop cocktails or brunch, or both.

Crumpler, Smith St

Brunswick Street Bookstore BOOKS

39 Map p106, B2

Lovely store with knowledgeable staff and a good selection of children's books. (☎03-9416 1030; www.brunswick streetbookstore.com; 305 Brunswick St, Fitzroy; ⏰10am-9pm; 🚋11)

Crumpler FASHION & ACCESSORIES

40 Map p106, C5

Crumpler's bike-courier bags – designed by two former couriers looking for a bag they could hold their beer in while cycling home – are what started it all. The brand's durable, practical designs now extend to bags for cameras,

laptops and iPads, and can be found around the world. (☎03-9417 5338; www.crumpler.com; 87 Smith St, Fitzroy; ⏰10am-6pm Mon-Sat, to 5pm Sun; 🚋86)

Obüs FASHION & ACCESSORIES

41 Map p106, C5

Melbourne-based designer Kylie Zerbst set up Obüs over 15 years ago with this, her first store. Known for bright geometric patterns and soft bamboo-cotton travel essentials, the clothing is sophisticated yet fun and offers pieces that get you from work to going out without a change. (☎03-9416 0012; www.obus.com.au; 226 Gertrude St, Fitzroy; ⏰10am-6pm Mon-Sat, 11am-5pm Sun; 🚋86)

Top Sights
Abbotsford Convent & Around

Getting There

🚗 Head east down Johnston St, turn right at Clarke St then left into Heliers St.

🚌 200, 207

🚃 Victoria Park

The nuns are long gone at this former convent, which dates back to 1861; so don't worry, no one will ask if you've been to mass lately. Today its rambling collection of ecclesiastic architecture is home to a thriving arts community of galleries, studios, cafes and bars, spread over nearly 7 hectares of riverside land. The adjoining Collingwood Children's Farm has a range of frolicking farm animals that kids can help feed, while Yarra Bend park makes for a lovely scenic bike ride or walk.

Convent Bakery

Markets

Shirt & Skirt Market (www.shirtandskirtmarkets.com.au; ☻10am-4pm 3rd Sun of month) on the third Sunday each month is the place to buy limited-run clothes and accessories from emerging designers. There's the Slow Food Market every fourth Saturday, and in summer the popular Supper Market on Friday nights, featuring food stalls and live music.

Collingwood Children's Farm

The inner city melts away at rustic, riverside **Collingwood Children's Farm** (www.farm.org.au; adult/child/family $10/5/20; ☻9.15am-4.30pm; 🚌200, 207, 🚉Victoria Park), a retreat that's beloved not just by kids. As well as farm animals to help feed, there are rambling gardens and grounds for picnicking on warm days. The monthly farmers market is a local highlight.

Yarra Bend Park

Backing onto the Convent, the Yarra River flows through scenic bushland with plenty of birdlife, great walking, cycling and picnicking. At the end of Boathouse Rd, Studley Park Boathouse, accessed via suspension footbridge across the river, has a kiosk, restaurant, BBQs and canoes for hire.

☏03-9415 3600

www.abbotsfordconvent.com.au

1 St Heliers St, Abbotsford

tours $15

☻7.30am-10pm

🚌200, 207, 🚉Victoria Park

☑ Top Tips

▶ Tours of the complex are run at 2pm every Sunday.

▶ A nice alternative to public transport or scrambling for parking spots is to cycle along Yarra Bend bike path.

✖ Take a Break

Plenty of great foodie options here. Try not-for-profit **Lentil As Anything** (☏03-9419 6444; www.lentilasanything.com; by donation; ☻9am-9pm) for delicious vegetarian dishes and the **Convent Bakery** (☏03-9419 9426; www.conventbakery.com; mains $10-20; ☻7am-5pm), which bakes goodies in the original 1901 wood-fired masonry ovens.

Explore

Carlton & Around

Home to Melbourne's Italian community and the University of Melbourne, Carlton dishes up a heady mix of intellectual activity, espresso and excellent food. You'll see the *tricolori* unfurled with characteristic passion come soccer finals and the Grand Prix. Surrounded by North Melbourne, hip East Brunswick and leafy North Carlton, this area is home to some big attractions like the Melbourne Museum and the zoo.

The Sights in a Day

☀ Coffee drinkers are spoilt for choice in this area. For your morning brew head to **Seven Seeds** (p133) or **Market Lane** (p135), both regarded as among the city's finest roasters. Otherwise head to Lygon St for traditional espresso at **Tiamo** (p133), one of Lygon St's originals. While you're here duck into **Museo Italiano** (p128) to get informed on the area's Italian history, then browse for books at **Readings** (p136).

☀ After a lunch of authentic thin-crust pizza from **D.O.C Pizza & Mozarella Bar** (p130), start your afternoon of sightseeing at Australia's oldest **zoo** (p128), established in 1862. Catch a tram towards the city to Nicholson St to admire the World Heritage-listed **Royal Exhibition Building** (p124), a striking art nouveau gem. Next door is the impressive **Melbourne Museum** (p122), which has a varied and accessible collection, including good coverage on Indigenous Australia.

☾ Return to Lygon St and **D.O.C Espresso** (p130) for a negroni *aperitivo* and complimentary snacks. For dinner, stick with Italian and try Venetian tapas at **Heartattack and Vine** (p130) or opt for a Lebanese meal at **Abla's** (p131) before enjoying quality indie theatre at **La Mama** (p135) or art-house flicks at **Cinema Nova** (p132). Don't miss a gelato from **Pidapipo** (p132).

◉ Top Sights

Melbourne Museum (p122)

Royal Exhibition Building (p124)

♥ Best of Melbourne

Eating

DOC Pizza & Mozzarella Bar (p130)

Pidapipo (p132)

Brunetti (p132)

Shopping

Readings (p136)

Gewürzhaus (p136)

Getting There

🚋 **Tram** For Lygon St, Carlton, trams 1 and 6 will take you past the university and to the corner of Lygon and Elgin Sts, within reach of the best restaurants and shops. The main tram to North Melbourne from the city is the 57 (from Elizabeth St).

🚆 **Train** The best way to get to Melbourne Zoo is to take the Upfield line to Royal Park station, which is positioned right outside the zoo's northern entrance.

Top Sights
Melbourne Museum

This museum provides a grand sweep of Victoria's natural and cultural histories, with exhibitions covering everything from dinosaur fossils and giant squid specimens to the taxidermy hall, a 3D volcano and an open-air forest atrium of Victorian flora. Become immersed in the legend of champion racehorse and national hero Phar Lap in the Marvellous Melbourne exhibition. The excellent Bunjilaka, on the ground floor, presents Indigenous Australian stories and history told through objects and Aboriginal voices with state-of-the-art technology. There's also an Imax cinema on site.

👁 Map p126, G5

www.museumvictoria.com.au

11 Nicholson St, Carlton

adult $14, child & student free, exhibitions extra

🕐 10am-5pm

🚌 Tourist Shuttle, 🚃 City Circle, 86, 96, 🚇 Parliament

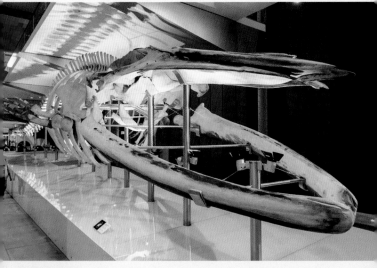

Blue whale skeleton

Bunjilaka Aboriginal Cultural Centre

The First Peoples permanent exhibition at the Bunjilaka Aboriginal Cultural Centre presents Indigenous Australian stories and history told through objects and Aboriginal voices with state-of-the-art technology. Highlights of the exhibition include the traditional possum skin cloaks, Bunjil's wings – a kinetic sculptural audiovisual installation – and the Deep Listening space, where you can hear Koorie people speak about their culture and share personal stories.

Taxidermy Hall

This impressive hall houses a large number of taxidermied animals set over different levels and you can peer down on them all from above. Here you can see Sam the Koala, who made headlines after footage was released of a firefighter giving her water and rescuing her during the devastating 2009 Black Saturday bushfires. She died afterwards and became the symbol of the loss from the fires.

Melbourne Gallery

The permanent Melbourne Story exhibition features around 1200 objects that help you delve into the city's history and get a sense of its personality. Walk through the history of Little Lonsdale St and check out the schoolboy costume of Angus Young of famous Australian rock band AC/DC. In this gallery you'll also find the museum's most popular display, the taxidermied Phar Lap, Australia's national hero and most loved racehorse of all time.

☑ **Top Tips**

▶ You can avoid any lengthy queues by buying your tickets online in advance on the museum website.

▶ Join a free guided tour of the museum's highlights; ask for the schedule as times can change daily.

▶ You'll need at least half a day to explore the museum.

▶ If you plan on visiting the Imax theatre next door, buy a combined ticket at the museum for a discount.

✘ **Take a Break**

A convenient option for a quick bite is the museum's on-site cafe on the ground floor, though it can get busy. Otherwise head to the ultracontemporary **Assembly** (www. assemblystore.com; 60 Pelham St, Carlton; ⏱7am-4pm Mon-Fri, from 9am Sat; 🛜; 🚍Tourist Shuttle, 🚋1, 3, 5, 6, 16, 64, 67, 72), a 10 minute walk away, for speciality filtered coffee and artisan teas complemented by delicious pastries.

Top Sights
Royal Exhibition Building

Built for the International Exhibition in 1880 and winning Unesco World Heritage status in 2004, this beautiful Victorian edifice symbolises the glory days of the Industrial Revolution, the British Empire and 19th-century Melbourne's economic supremacy. It was the first building to fly the Australian flag, and Australia's first parliament was held here in 1901; it now hosts everything from trade fairs to car shows.

👁 Map p126, G5

📞 13 11 02

www.museumvictoria.com.au/reb

9 Nicholson St, Carlton

tours adult/child $10/7

🚌 Tourist Shuttle, 🚋 City Circle, 86, 96, 🚇 Parliament

The Architecture

Designed by architect Joseph Reed, the stunning Royal Exhibition Building is the only surviving Great Hall that was originally used for a 19th-century international exhibition and is still used for the same purpose to this day. Admire the round-arched Rundbogenstil architecture, a style which combines elements from Romanesque, Lombardic, Byzantine and Italian Renaissance buildings. The design of the dome was influenced by Brunelleschi's 15th-century cathedral in Florence. In 2004 the Royal Exhibition Building became the first building in Australia to be given World Heritage listing.

The Interior

The inside of the building is equally as impressive as its exterior, with extensive decorative paintwork throughout and exquisite detail. In the spaces where the arches join the cornices, you can see intricate lunettes with sculptural details that represent Peace, War, Federation and Government. The interior underwent a massive restoration project in 1994 to bring it back to its 1901 colour scheme.

Carlton Gardens

The surrounding gardens, also part of the World Heritage listing, are a popular, peaceful spot for nearby office workers, locals and tourists. The gardens are bordered by Victoria, Rathdowne, Carlton and Nicholson Sts, and are a great example of Victorian landscaping with a network of wide tree-lined avenues, a beautiful fountain and native wildlife.

☑ Top Tips

▶ The only way to see inside is by tour or on entry to an exhibition.

▶ Tours of the building run most days, leaving Melbourne Museum at 2pm ($5).

✗ Take a Break

Pack some picnic goodies before you set off; the surrounding Carlton Gardens provide the perfect spot for a lunchtime break.

For something more upmarket, try nearby Epocha (p131) set in a grand Victorian terrace.

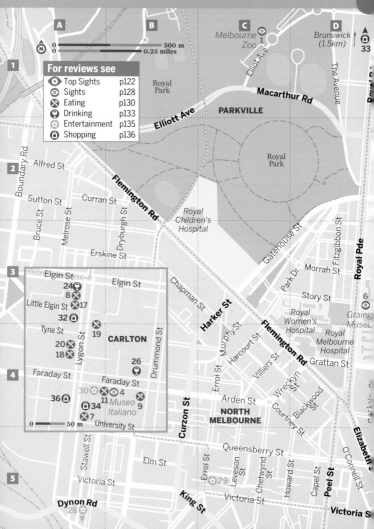

A B C D

Melbourne Zoo C 1

Brunswick (1.5km) D 33

N 0 500 m
0 0.25 miles

For reviews see

⦿	Top Sights	p122
⊙	Sights	p128
⊗	Eating	p130
🍺	Drinking	p133
⭐	Entertainment	p135
🛍	Shopping	p136

Royal Park

Elliott Ave

Macarthur Rd

PARKVILLE

The Avenue

Boundary Rd

Alfred St

Sutton St

Curran St

Flemington Rd

Royal Park

Bruce St

Melrose St

Dryburgh St

Erskine St

Royal Children's Hospital

Gatehouse St

Park Dr

Morrah St

Story St

Royal Pde

6 Graing Muse

Elgin St

Elgin St

Chapman St

Harker St

Fitzgibbon St

24 ⊙
8 ⊙ ⊗17
Little Elgin St
32 🛍

Tyne St

20 ⊗
18 ⊗

Lygon St

⊗ 19

CARLTON

Drummond St

26 🍺

Murphy St

Royal Women's Hospital

Harcourt St

Villiers St

Flemington Rd

Royal Melbourne Hospital

Grattan St

Wreckyn St

Faraday St

36 🛍

30 ⊗
⊗ 4
11 ⊗9
Faraday St
Museo Italiano
🍺34
⊗ 7

University St

0 50 m

Curzon St

Errol St

Arden St

NORTH MELBOURNE

Courtney St

Blackwood St

Stawell St

Elm St

Victoria St

Queensberry St

Errol St

Leveson St

Chetwynd St

Howard St

Capel St

O'Connell St

Peel St

Elizabeth

Dynon Rd

28 ⭐

⭐29

King St

Victoria St

Victoria S

Sights

Melbourne Zoo   ZOO

1 ◎ Map p126, C1

Established in 1861, this compact zoo is the oldest in Australia and the third oldest in the world. It remains one of the city's most popular attractions and it continues to innovate, recently becoming the world's first carbon-neutral zoo. Set in prettily landscaped gardens, the zoo's enclosures aim to simulate the animals' natural habitats and give them the option to hide if they want to (the gorillas and the tigers are particularly good at playing hard to get). (☑1300 966 784; www.zoo.org.au; Elliott Ave, Parkville; adult/child $33/17, child weekends & holidays free; ☉8am-5pm; ♦; ☒Royal Park)

Ian Potter Museum of Art   GALLERY

2 ◎ Map p126, E3

The Ian Potter Museum of Art manages Melbourne University's extensive art collection, which ranges from antiquities to contemporary Australian work. It's a thoughtfully designed space and always has an exciting exhibition program. Pick up the *Sculpture on Campus* map here for a walking tour taking in Melbourne Uni's sculptures, set amid heritage-listed buildings. (☑03-8344 5148; www.art-museum.unimelb.edu.au; Melbourne University, 800 Swanston St, Parkville; ad-

mission free; ☉10am-5pm Tue-Fri, noon-5pm Sat & Sun; ☒1, 3, 5, 6, 16, 64, 67, 72)

Melbourne General Cemetery   CEMETERY

3 ◎ Map p126, F2

Melbourne has been burying its dead in this cemetery since 1852. It's worth a stroll to see the final resting place of three Australian prime ministers, the ill-fated explorers Burke and Wills, Walter Lindrum's billiard-table tombstone and a shrine to Elvis erected by fans. Check the website about guided day and night tours. (☑03-9349 3014; www.mgc.smct.org.au; College Cres, Parkville; ☉8am-6pm Apr-Sep, to 8pm Oct-Mar; ☒1, 6)

Museo Italiano   MUSEUM

4 ◎ Map p126, B4

Telling the story of Melbourne's Italian community, this museum offers a good starting point to put the history of Lygon St into both historical and contemporary context. (☑03-9349 9000; www.museoitaliano.com.au; 199 Faraday St, Carlton; admission free; ☉10am-5pm Tue-Fri, noon-5pm Sat; ☒Tourist Shuttle, ☒1, 6)

University of Melbourne   UNIVERSITY

5 ◎ Map p126, E3

The esteemed University of Melbourne was established in 1853 and remains one of Australia's most prestigious universities. Its blend of Victorian Gothic stone buildings, midcentury international-style

Melbourne Zoo

towers and postmodern showpieces provides a snapshot of changing architectural aspirations. The campus sprawls from Carlton through to the neighbouring suburb of Parkville, and its extensive grounds house the university colleges. Most notable is the Walter Burley Griffin–designed Newman College. Pick up a *Sculpture on Campus* map from the Ian Potter Museum of Art (p128). (☎03-8344 4000; www.unimelb.edu.au; Grattan St, Carlton; 🚊1, 3, 5, 6, 16, 64, 67, 72)

Grainger Museum MUSEUM

6 ◎ Map p126, D3

A tribute to one of Australia's great musical exports, this museum housed in an art deco building lays bare the fascinating life of Percy Grainger. Leaving Australia aged nine, Grainger became an internationally renowned composer and pianist in Europe and the USA, as well as a forerunner in experimental music. Exhibits from all points of his life are on display, from his sound machines to a collection of fetish whips. (☎03-8344 5270; www.grainger.unimelb.edu.au; Gate 13, Melbourne University, Royal Pde, Parkville; admission free; ☺noon-4pm Sun-Fri; 🚊19)

Eating

D.O.C. Espresso ITALIAN $$

7 ✕ Map p126, A4

Run by third-generation Italian Australians, authentic D.O.C. has breathed
new life into Lygon St. The espresso
bar features homemade pasta specials,
Italian microbrewery beers and *aperitivo* time (4pm to 7pm), when you can
enjoy a negroni with complimentary
nibble board. (✆03-9347 8482; www.
docgroup.net; 326 Lygon St, Carlton; mains
$12-20; ✪7.30am-late Mon-Sat, 8am-late
Sun; ☐Tourist Shuttle, ☐1, 6)

Heartattack and Vine ITALIAN $

8 ✕ Map p126, A3

Heartattack and Vine is a relaxed
space with a neighbourhood feel
all centred on a long wooden bar.
Drop in for a coffee morning or
night, prop up at the bar for an
Aperol spritz or glass of wine, grab
a brekky pastry or prawn brioche
roll for lunch, or spend the evening
sampling the *cicchetti*, a Venetian
take on tapas. (✆03-9005 8674; www.

heartattackandvine.com.au; 329 Lygon St,
Carlton; ✪7am-11pm Mon-Fri, from 8am Sat
& Sun; 🛜; ☐Tourist Shuttle, ☐1,6)

D.O.C. Pizza & Mozzarella Bar PIZZA $$

9 ✕ Map p126, B4

D.O.C. has jumped on the Milanese-
led mozzarella-bar trend and serves
up the milky-white balls – your choice
of local cow or imported *buffala* – as
entrees, in salads or atop fabulous
pizzas. Pizza toppings include bitter-
sweet *cicoria* (chicory) and lemon,
and wild mushrooms and truffle oil;
the litmus-test margherita gets rave
reviews. (✆03-9347 2998; www.docgroup.
net; 295 Drummond St, Carlton; pizzas $17-
25; ✪5pm-late Mon-Wed, noon-late Fri-Sun;
☐Tourist Shuttle, ☐1, 6)

Babajan TURKISH $$

10 ✕ Map p126, H1

For a small corner cafe, Babajan
whips up some pretty big Turkish flavours. Kirsty Chiaplias, who runs the
show, has culinary cred going back
years from working with noteworthy
chefs such as Gordon Ramsay. Drop
in for a deliciously flaky *borek* or a
grain-and-pulse-filled salad, or feast
on cumin-and-mint-rubbed lamb
shanks or a crab and halloumi ome-
lette. (✆03-9388 9814; www.babajan.com.
au; 713 Nicholson St, North Carlton; mains
$12-26; ✪Tues-Fri 7am-7pm, Sat & Sun to
5pm; ☐96)

☑ Top Tip

Dining on Lygon Street

Avoid the spruikers on Lygon St
and keep travelling north past
Grattan St for the most authentic
Italian eateries; some lovely cafes
and restaurants line the street here
and beyond.

Shakahari

VEGETARIAN $$

11 ⊗ Map p126, A4

Shakahari's limited, seasonal menu reflects both Asian and European influences, and dishes are made using great produce. Established over 40 years ago, and bedecked with a wonderful collection of Asian antiques, Shakahari takes its mission seriously. If the weather is in your favour, ask to be seated in the palm-fringed courtyard. (☑03-9347 3848; www.shakahari.com.au; 201 Faraday St, Carlton; mains $19-22; ⊙noon-3pm & 6-9.30pm Mon-Fri, 6-10.30pm Sat & Sun; ☑; ☒Tourist Shuttle, ☒1, 3, 5, 6, 16, 64, 67, 72)

Small Victories

CAFE $$

12 ⊗ Map p126, G2

Not your ordinary posh North Carlton cafe, Small Victories is big on DIY, preparing and smoking its own smallgoods, churning its own butter and making pastas from scratch. It rounds it all off with single-origin coffee and craft beers. (☑03-9347 4064; www.small-victoriescafe.com.au; 617 Rathdowne St, North Carlton; smallgoods from $13; ⊙8am-5pm Mon-Sat, 9am-5pm Sun; ☒1, 6)

Abla's

LEBANESE $$

13 ⊗ Map p126, G3

The kitchen here is steered by Abla Amad, whose authentic, flavour-packed food has inspired a whole generation of local Lebanese chefs. The banquet menu (from $60) is compulsory on Friday and Saturday nights.

Q Local Life

Princes Park

Joggers and walkers pound the 3.2km gravel path around the perimeter of the **park** (Princes Park Dr, North Carlton; ☒19), while cricket, soccer and dog walking fill up the centre. It's the former home of the Carlton Football Club (and its current training ground).

BYO wine Monday to Thursday. (☑03-9347 0006; www.ablas.com.au; 109 Elgin St, Carlton; mains $28-30; ⊙6-10pm Mon-Sat, noon-3pm Thu & Fri; ☒1, 6, 96)

Kaprica

PIZZA $$

14 ⊗ Map p126, E5

Tucked away opposite Lincoln Sq is this intimate, rustic spot with white-linen-covered tables, handwritten menus and delicious pizzas. Look for the tables out the front. (☑03-9347 1138; 19 Lincoln Sq South, Carlton; pizza $17-21; ⊙10am-10pm; ☒1, 3, 5, 6, 16, 64, 67, 72)

Epocha

EUROPEAN $$

15 ⊗ Map p126, F5

Set within a grand Victorian double-storey terrace dating from 1884, elegant Epocha creates an interesting mix of Greek- and English-inspired dishes that's reflective of each of the co-owners' successes in previous restaurants. It all comes together beautifully on the $68 sharing menu. Head upstairs for fantastic cocktails at Hannah's Bar. (☑03-9036 4949;

www.epocha.com.au; 49 Rathdowne St, Carlton; small/large sharing plates from $16/27; ⊘noon-3pm & 5.30-10pm Tue-Sat, noon-3pm Sun; ⛴City Circle, 30)

Longhorn Saloon

AMERICAN $$

16 🍴 Map p126, G3

Longhorn Saloon is an upmarket Wild West saloon–style restaurant-bar with lots of pressed copper, exposed brick, dark wood and low lighting. The menu features Southern-style flavours, from steaks cooked on the wood-fire grill to a brisket Reuben sandwich and a side of jalapeño-spiced mac 'n' cheese. Pair it with a hoppy US IPA or a classic Dark 'n' Stormy cocktail. (☏03-9348 4794; www.longhornsaloon.com.au; 118 Elgin St, Carlton; mains $16-44; ⊘from 5pm Tue-Thu, noon-late Fri-Sun; ⛴1, 6)

Milk the Cow

EUROPEAN $$

17 🍴 Map p126, A3

When a cheese craving strikes, head to licensed fromagerie Milk the Cow for baked camembert with a crusty baguette or a farmer's board of

---

Local Life

Cinema Nova

See the latest in art-house, docos and foreign films at this **cinema** (☏03-9347 5331; www.cinemanova. com.au; 380 Lygon St, Carlton; ⛴Tourist Shuttle, ⛴1, 6), a locals' favourite. Cheap Monday screenings ($7 before 4pm, $9 after 4pm).

---

country-style bites. The electric milking chandeliers are a talking point, as is the giant glass cabinet filled with more than 150 unique, hard-to-find cheeses from all over the world. (☏03-9348 4771; www.milkthecow.com.au; 323 Lygon St, Carlton; cheeseboards from $27, flights & fondue from $17; ⊘noon-late; ⛴1, 6)

Pidapipo

GELATO $

18 🍴 Map p126, A4

Pidapipo is the perfect precinema, pretheatre, postpizza – whenever! – treat when you're hanging out on Lygon St. Owner Lisa Valmorbida learned from the best in the world at the Carpigiani Gelato University and now whips up her own handmade creations on-site from local and imported Italian ingredients. (☏03-9347 4596; http://pidapipo.com.au; 299 Lygon St, Carlton; 1 scoop $4.50; ⊘noon-11pm; ⛴Tourist Shuttle, ⛴1, 6)

Brunetti

ITALIAN $

19 🍴 Map p126, A4

Bustling from dawn to midnight, Brunetti is a mini–Roman empire with a drool-inducing display of cakes and sweets. It's famous for its coffee, granitas and authentic *pasticceria* (pastries), and also does a menu of pizzas, pastas and panini. (☏03-9347 2801; www.brunetti.com.au; 380 Lygon St, Carlton; panini around $10, mains from $17; ⊘cafe 6am-11pm Sun-Thu, to midnight Fri & Sat; 🛜; ⛴Tourist Shuttle, ⛴1, 6, 96)

Old Arts, University of Melbourne (p128)

Tiamo

ITALIAN $$

20  Map p126, A4

When you've had enough of pressed, siphoned, Slayer-machined, poured-over, filtered and plunged coffee, head here to one of Lygon St's original Italian cafe-restaurants. There's the laughter and relaxed joie de vivre that only a well-established restaurant can offer. Great pastas and pizza, too. Also has the upmarket Tiamo 2 next door. (☑03-9347 5759; www.tiamo.com.au; 303 Lygon St, Carlton; mains $15-26; ☺6am-10.30pm; ☐Tourist Shuttle, ☐1, 6)

Drinking

Seven Seeds

CAFE

21 Map p126, E5

The most spacious location in the Seven Seeds coffee empire, this rather out-of-the-way warehouse cafe has plenty of room to store your bike and sip a splendid coffee. Public cuppings are held 9am Friday. It also owns **Traveller** (2/14 Crossley St; bagels $7-10; ☺7am-5pm Mon-Fri; ☐86, 96) and **Brother Baba Budan** (359 Little Bourke St; ☺7am-5pm Mon-Sat, 9am-5pm Sun; ☎; ☐Melbourne Central) cafes in the CBD. (☑03-9347 8664; www.sevenseeds.com. au; 114 Berkeley St, Carlton; ☺7am-5pm Mon-Sat, 8am-5pm Sun; ☐19, 59)

Town Hall Hotel

Sure, it's more than a bit grungy, but that's part of the charm of this endearingly unfussy local **hotel** (📞03-9328 1983; www.townhallhotelnorthmelbourne.com.au; 33 Errol St, North Melbourne; ⏱4pm-1am Mon-Thu, noon-1am Fri & Sat, noon-11pm Sun; 🚊57) that's festooned with rock iconography (Bowie and Iggy feature prominently). Other more traditionally religious figures adorn the rear dining room, too. There's a beer garden, too. There's often live music from Thursday to Sunday; otherwise they'll be spinning some classic vinyl.

Wide Open Road   CAFE

22 🚇 Map p126, E1

Wide Open in name translates to wide open in space at this inviting converted-warehouse cafe-roastery just off hectic Sydney Rd. There's plenty of elbow room at the communal tables, where you can tuck into dishes from a refreshingly inventive menu. Try the fish-finger sandwich with pickled cucumbers while sipping a Bathysphere house-blend espresso or weekly-changing filter coffee. (📞03-9010 9298; http://wideopenroad.com.au; 274 Barkly St, Brunswick; ⏱7am-4pm Mon-Fri, to 5pm Sat, 8am-5pm Sun; 🛜; 🚊19, 🚉Jewell)

Gerald's Bar   WINE BAR

23 🚇 Map p126, G1

Wine by the glass is democratically selected at this neighbourhood favourite, and they spin some fine vintage vinyl from behind the curved wooden bar. Gerald himself is out the back preparing to feed you whatever he feels like on the day with produce sourced mainly from local producers. (📞03-9349 4748; http://geraldsbar.com.au; 386 Rathdowne St, North Carlton; ⏱5-11pm Mon-Sat; 🚊1, 6)

Jimmy Watson's   WINE BAR

24 🚇 Map p126, A3

If this Robin Boyd–designed mid-century building had ears, there'd be a few generations of writers and academics in trouble. Keep it tidy at Watson's wine bar with something nice by the glass, go a bottle of dry and dry (vermouth and ginger ale) and settle in the leafy courtyard, or head up to the Wolf's Lair rooftop for cocktails with a view. (📞03-9347 3985; www.jimmywatsons.com.au; 333 Lygon St, Carlton; ⏱wine bar 11am-11pm, Wolf's Lair rooftop 4-11pm; 🚌Tourist Shuttle, 🚊1, 6)

Lincoln   PUB

25 🚇 Map p126, F5

A bit posher than your average old Carlton boozer, the Lincoln hints at historical charm with art-deco features and a dark-wood curved bar. It offers an impressive wine list and a rotating selection of craft beer on tap, alongside the classic Carlton Draught, of course. The kitchen does gastropub meals (coffee-cured salmon, whole baby snapper) and does them well. (☎03-9347 4666; http://hotellincoln.com.au; 91 Cardigan St, Carlton; ⊙noon-11pm Sun-Thu, to midnight Fri & Sat; 🚋1, 3, 5, 6, 16, 64, 67, 72)

Market Lane
COFFEE

26 🚇 Map p126, B4

This northside outpost of Market Lane (p44) occupies the tiny front room of a terrace house where you can sidle up to the takeaway window or grab a stool street-side as you sip one of its excellent brews. (http://marketlane.com.au; 176 Faraday St, Carlton; ⊙7am-4pm Mon-Sat, from 8am Sun; 🚋Tourist Shuttle, 🚋1, 6)

Queensberry Pourhouse
CAFE

27 🚇 Map p126, E5

A relaxed corner coffeehouse inspired by American diners, where the filter coffee is bottomless and lingering is welcomed – it's perfect for students at nearby Melbourne Uni. The beans are roasted on-site and there's a short menu of tasty food; try the mushroom toasties or the house-made granola. (☎03-9347 1277; www.queensberryph.com.au; 210 Queensberry St, Carlton; ⊙7am-4.30pm; 🚋1, 3, 5, 6, 16, 64, 67, 72)

Entertainment

Festival Hall
CONCERT VENUE

28 ⭐ Map p126, A5

This former boxing stadium – aka 'Festering Hall' (especially on hot summer nights) – is a fave for live international acts. The Beatles played here in 1964. (☎03-9329 9699; www.festivalhall.com.au; 300 Dudley St, West Melbourne; 🚋220, 🚉North Melbourne)

Comic's Lounge
COMEDY

29 ⭐ Map p126, C5

There's stand-up featuring Melbourne's best-known funny people most nights of the week here. If you like to live dangerously, Tuesday's when professional comedians try out new material. Admission prices vary. (☎03-9348 9488; www.thecomicslounge.com.au; 26 Errol St, North Melbourne; ⊙dinner/show from 6.30/8pm Mon-Sat; 🚋57)

La Mama
THEATRE

30 ⭐ Map p126, A4

La Mama is historically significant in Melbourne's theatre scene. This tiny, intimate forum produces new Australian works and experimental theatre, and has a reputation for developing emerging playwrights. It's a ramshackle building with an open-air bar. Shows also run at its larger Courthouse theatre at 349 Drummond St, so check tickets carefully for the correct location. (☎03-9347 6948; www.lamama.com.au; 205 Faraday St, Carlton; tickets $10-25; ⊙box office 10.30am-5pm Mon-Fri, 2-3pm Sat & Sun; 🚍Tourist Shuttle, 🚊1, 6)

Last Chance Rock & Roll Bar

LIVE MUSIC

31 ⭐ Map p126, D5

The Public Bar, a much-loved local institution, closed recently and Last Chance took over in the same spirit – it's clear there's been no spit-and-polish here and it's just as perfectly divey as ever. Live bands play most nights and lean towards the punk genre. (☎03-9329 9888; www.thelastchance.com.au; 238 Victoria St, North Melbourne; ⊙4pm-late Mon-Thu, noon-7am Fri & Sat, noon-11pm Sun; 🚊19, 57, 55)

Shopping

Readings

BOOKS

32 🔒 Map p126, A3

A potter around this defiantly prosperous indie bookshop can occupy an entire afternoon if you're so inclined. There's a dangerously loaded (and good-value) specials table and switched-on, helpful staff. Just next door is its speciality children's store. (www.readings.com.au; 309 Lygon St, Carlton; ⊙9am-11pm Mon-Sat, 10am-9pm Sun; 🚍Tourist Shuttle, 🚊1, 6)

Mr Kitly

HOMEWARES

33 🔒 Map p126, D1

Head up the narrow stairs to a treasure trove of carefully curated homewares, indoor plants and accessories with a heavy Japanese influence. Get lost in time in this beautiful store as you covet everything from Hasami porcelain and copper gardening tools to Lithuanian bed linen and self-watering pot plants by Decor in pretty pastel colours. (☎03-9078 7357; http://mrkitly.com.au; 381 Sydney Rd, Brunswick; ⊙11am-6pm Mon & Wed-Fri, to 4pm Sat & Sun; 🚊19, 🚉Brunswick)

Gewürzhaus

FOOD

34 🔒 Map p126, A4

Set up by two enterprising young German women, this store is a chef's dream with its displays of spices from around the world, including Indigenous Australian blends, flavoured salts and sugars. It has high-quality cooking accessories and gifts, and cooking classes, too. There's a city store inside the Block Arcade (p31). (☎03-9348 4815; www.gewurzhaus.com.au; 342 Lygon St, Carlton; ⊙10am-6pm Mon-Sat, 11am-5pm Sun; 🚍Tourist Shuttle, 🚊1, 6)

Lab Organics

COSMETICS

35 🔒 Map p126, G2

Right at home on this boutique stretch of Rathdowne St, Lab has a carefully selected range of organic skincare products, fragrances and

Readings

beauty accessories made locally and sourced from around the globe. Products for men, too. (http://thelab organics.com.au; 360 Rathdowne St, North Carlton; ⏲10am-6pm Wed-Fri, to 5.30pm Sat-Tue; 🚋1, 6)

Poppy Shop   TOYS

36 🔒 Map p126, A4

A Carlton stalwart, tiny Poppy is a riot of intriguing toys, decorative objects and other happy-making paraphernalia. From beautiful hand-crafted wooden toys to mechanical wind-up robots and tiny kewpie dolls for a few dollars, there's plenty to keep whole families entertained (if you can all fit in the shop at the same time). (☎03-9347 6302; http://poppyshop.com.au; 283 Lygon St, Carlton; ⏲9.30am-5.30pm Mon-Thu, to 6pm Fri, to 5pm Sat, 11am-4pm Sun; 🚋Tourist Shuttle, 🚋1, 3, 5, 6, 16, 64, 67, 72)

Explore

St Kilda

St Kilda is Melbourne's slightly tattered bohemian heart and a place featured in countless songs, plays, novels, TV series and films. Starting life as a 19th-century seaside resort, St Kilda has played many roles: post-war Jewish enclave, red-light district, punk-rocker hub and real-estate hotspot. It's a hypnotic jumble of mansions, seedy side streets, wine bars, pubs, rickety roller-coasters and nostalgia-inducing theatres.

The Sights in a Day

☀ Start in East St Kilda along Carlisle St to soak up its Eastern European heritage, with fresh bagels at **Glick's** (p144) and a visit to the **Jewish Museum of Australia** (p143) to put the area into context. Then head along Acland St for a morning tea of *kugelhopf* (marble cake) at the iconic **Monarch Cake Shop** (p145).

☀ Spend the afternoon strolling the **St Kilda Foreshore** (p140), and perhaps get out on the water with kitesurfing or a stand-up paddle-boarding lesson. For a drink at sunset head to **Republica** (p149), directly on the beach.

☾ As soon as the sun goes down, St Kilda steps up a gear as revellers descend from all over Melbourne for a debaucherous night out. Escape the madness by enjoying a seafood dinner with bay views at **Stokehouse** (p145) before drinks at **Bar Di Stasio** (p149). Afterwards, be spoiled for choice of craft beer at the **Local Taphouse** (p149) then catch a flick at the **Astor** (p150) or a gig at the **Prince** (p150).

👁 Top Sights

St Kilda Foreshore (p140)

💜 Best of Melbourne

Eating

Monk Bodhi Dharma (p146)

Stokehouse (p145)

Attica (p144)

Claypots (p145)

Lentil as Anything (p146)

Drinking

Local Taphouse (p149)

Getting There

🚊 **Tram** From the city, trams 1, 3a, 12, 16 and 96 reach St Kilda. Tram 12 terminates at Fitzroy St, while trams 1, 3a, 16 and 96 also reach the Esplanade and Acland St. Trams 3a and 16 connect St Kilda to Balaclava's main shopping and cafe strip, Carlisle St.

🚆 **Train** Sandringham-line trains stop at Balaclava station, right on Carlisle St. Trains do not service St Kilda.

Top Sights
St Kilda Foreshore

Despite the palm-fringed promenades and golden stretch of sand, St Kilda's seaside appeal is more Brighton, England, than Venice, LA. The kiosk at the end of St Kilda Pier is as much about the journey as the destination: the pier offers a knockout panorama of the Melbourne skyline. During summer Port Phillip EcoCentre runs a range of tours, including urban wildlife walks and coastal discovery walks, and offers information on the little-penguin colony that lives in the breakwater behind the pier's kiosk.

👁 Map p142, A3

Jacka Blvd, St Kilda

🚃 3, 12, 16, 96

St Kilda Foreshore

Historic Landmarks

St Kilda Pier (Jacka Blvd; 🚋3, 12, 16, 96) is a much-loved icon that's great for stroll. At its end sits the quaint pavillion kiosk, which burned down in 2003 (a year short of its centenary), and was faithfully restored in 2006. Other striking architecture along the promenade includes heritage-listed **Palais Theatre** (☎03-9525 3240, tickets 136 100; Lower Esplanade; 🚋3, 16, 96), built c 1927 and the Moorish-style St Kilda Sea Baths, c 1910.

Luna Park

Opened in 1912, **Luna Park** (☎03-9525 5033; www.lunapark.com.au; 18 Lower Esplanade; single ride adult/child $11/10, unlimited rides $50/40; ⊙hours vary; 🚋3, 16, 96) retains the feel of an old-style amusement park, with creepy Mr Moon's gaping mouth swallowing you up as you enter. The heritage-listed 'Scenic Railway' is the oldest operating roller-coaster in the world. There's a beautifully baroque carousel with hand-painted horses, swans and chariots, and the full complement of gut-churning rides.

St Kilda Beach

Tourists may not flock to Melbourne for its city beaches, but come hot weather St Kilda's the place to be. Cool off with a swim in the bay, kiteboarding (all the rage November to April), stand-up paddleboarding or windsurfing.

Penguins

The breakwater near St Kilda pier is home to a colony of little penguins that have, incredibly, chosen the city's most crowded suburb in which to reside. For the best chance of catching a glimpse, head to the pier just after sunset.

☑ **Top Tips**

▶ The Esplanade Market (p150), held each Sunday, has a kilometre of trestle tables joined end-to-end with individually crafted products from toys to organic soaps and metal sculptures.

▶ Late November to mid-December Ben & Jerry's Openair Cinemas show recent releases and cult classics by the sea, with bar service and the option of renting blankets ($4) and bean-bag lounges ($9).

▶ Neighbouring Elwood Beach is a less busy and touristy alternative to St Kilda.

✕ **Take a Break**

Catch the ocean breeze over coffee and cake and enjoy unhindered bay and city views from historic St Kilda Pier kiosk. Grab breakfast or a sunset beer at Republica (p149). St Kilda's closest thing to a beach bar.

GREG BRAVE/SHUTTERSTOCK ©

St Kilda Botanical Gardens (p144)

Sights

Jewish Holocaust Centre

MUSEUM

1  Map p142, D4

Dedicated to the memory of the six million Jews who lost their lives during the Holocaust, this well-presented museum was set up by survivors as a sobering reminder of the atrocities they endured. Guided tours are available, often led by Holocaust survivors themselves. (☏03-9528 1985; www.jhc. org.au; 13-15 Selwyn St, Elsternwick; by donation; ⏰10am-4pm Mon-Thu, to 2pm Fri, noon-4pm Sun; 🚌67, 🚂Elsternwick)

Jewish Museum of Australia

MUSEUM

2  Map p142, D2

Interactive displays tell the history of Australia's Jewish community from the earliest days of European settlement, while permanent exhibitions celebrate Judaism's rich cycle of festivals and holy days. The museum also has a good curatorial reputation for its contemporary art exhibitions. By car, follow St Kilda Rd from St Kilda Junction, then turn left at Alma Rd. (☏03-9834 3600; www.jewishmuseum.com. au; 26 Alma Rd, St Kilda; adult/child/family $10/5/20; ⏰10am-4pm Tue-Thu, to 3pm Fri, to 5pm Sun, closed Jewish holy days; 🚌3, 67)

Linden New Art GALLERY

3 Map p142, B3

Housed in a wrought-iron-clad 1870s mansion, Linden mainly champions new contemporary art by midcareer artists. The annual postcard show (generally held from late October to January) is a highlight. (☑03-9534 0099; www.lindenarts.org; 26 Acland St, St Kilda; ☺11am-4pm Tue & Thu-Sun, to 8pm Wed; ☒3, 12, 16, 96)

St Kilda Botanical Gardens GARDENS

4 Map p142, C4

Taking pride of place on the southern line of the Barkly, Carlisle and Blessington St triangle, the Botanical Gardens are an unexpected haven from the St Kilda hustle. Wide gravel paths invite a leisurely stroll, and there are plenty of shady spots for sprawling on the open lawns. Features include local indigenous plants, a subtropical-rainforest conservatory

and a giant chessboard for large-scale plotting. (☑03-9209 6777; www.portphillip.vic. gov.au; cnr Blessington & Tennyson Sts, St Kilda; ☺sunrise-sunset, conservatory 10.30am-3.30pm Mon-Fri, sunrise-sunset Sat & Sun; ☒96)

Eating

Attica MODERN AUSTRALIAN $$$

5 Map p142, D4

The only Australian restaurant on the San Pellegrino World's Top 50 Restaurants list, Attica is home to prodigious Kiwi import Ben Shewry and his extraordinary culinary creations. Native ingredients shine in dishes like bunya bunya with salted red kangaroo, or bush-currant granité with lemon aspen and rosella flower. Reservations accepted three months ahead, on the first Wednesday of each month at 9am. Note that tables of two can go within a couple of hours, especially for Friday and Saturday nights. You'll have a better chance with a table for four or more, or trying for dinner midweek. It's also worth emailing or calling to check if availability isn't showing online. If driving, follow Brighton Rd south and turn left onto Glen Eira Rd. (☑03-9530 0111; www.attica.com.au; 74 Glen Eira Rd, Ripponlea; tasting menu $250; ☺6pm-late Tue-Sat; ☒67, ☒Ripponlea)

Cicciolina ITALIAN $$$

6 Map p142, C4

This hideaway of dark wood, subdued lighting and pencil sketches is a St Kilda institution. The menu is modern Italian, with dishes that might see tortellini paired beautifully with Persian feta, ricotta, pine nuts, lime zest, asparagus and burnt sage butter. Bookings only for lunch; for dinner, eat very early or while away your wait in the moody back bar. (☏03-9525 3333; www.cicciolinastkilda.com.au; 130 Acland St, St Kilda; mains lunch $18-30, dinner $27-45; ☉noon-10pm; ☐3, 16, 96)

Claypots
SEAFOOD $$

7 🍴 Map p142, C4

A local favourite, Claypots serves up fresh, share-style plates of seafood. Its namesake dish is available in a number of options, including a beautifully spiced Moroccan (mussels and fish fillet cooked with couscous, tomato, eggplant, harissa, zaatar and chickpeas). Get in early to both nab a seat and ensure the good stuff is still available, as hot items go fast. (☏03-9534 1282; www.facebook.com/claypotsstkilda; 213 Barkly St, St Kilda; claypots $20, mains $24-45; ☉noon-1am; ☐96)

Lau's Family Kitchen
CHINESE $$$

8 🍴 Map p142, B2

This polished nosh spot serves beautiful, home-style Cantonese with a few Sichuan surprises, including a seductive braised eggplant with spiced minced pork. Reserve for one of the two dinner sittings, and check out the elegant wall panels, made

Monarch Cake Shop

Monarch (☏03-9534 2972; www.monarchcakes.com.au; 103 Acland St, St Kilda; slice of cake from $5; ☉8am-9.30pm Sun-Thu, to 10pm Fri & Sat; ☐96) is a favourite among St Kilda's Eastern European cake shops, and its *kugelhopf* (marble cake), plum cake and Polish baked cheesecake can't be beaten. In business since 1934, the shop doesn't seem to have changed much, with a soft, old-time atmosphere and wonderful buttery aromas. It also does good coffee.

from 1930s kimonos. (☏03-8598 9880; www.lauskitchen.com.au; 4 Acland St, St Kilda; mains $26-45; ☉noon-3pm Mon-Fri, 12.30-3.30pm Sun, dinner sittings 6pm & 8pm daily; ☐16, 96)

Stokehouse
SEAFOOD $$$

9 🍴 Map p142, B3

After a devastating fire, the lauded Stokehouse is back, brighter and better than ever. Striking contemporary architecture and floor-to-ceiling bay views set the right tone for fresh, modern, seafood-centric dishes, not to mention a stuff-of-legend bombe Alaska. This is one of Melbourne's hottest restaurants, so always book ahead. (☏03-9525 5555; www.stokehouse.com.au; 30 Jacka Blvd, St Kilda; mains $36-42; ☉noon-3pm & 6pm-late; ☐3a, 16, 96)

I Carusi II

PIZZA $$

10 Map p142, C4

Located around the corner from the Acland St chaos, this casually elegant Italian is well loved for its thin-based pizzas. While quality isn't always consistent, the pizzas are smashing when they're done well. Check the board for creative pasta specials, and flaunt your sophistication by ordering a Cynar *spritz* – Venice's less-sweet take on the ubiquitous Aperol *spritz*. Bookings advised. (03-9593 6033; 231 Barkly St, St Kilda; pizza $19-26; 6-10pm Mon-Fri, from 5pm Sat & Sun; 3, 16, 96)

Lentil as Anything

VEGETARIAN $

11 Map p142, C4

Choosing from the vegetarian menu is easy. Deciding what to pay can be hard. This unique not-for-profit operation provides training and edu-cational opportunities for marginalised people, as well as tasty flesh-free grub. Whatever you pay for your meal goes towards helping new migrants, refugees, people with disabilities and the long-term unemployed. There are several branches, including one at Abbotsford Convent (p119). (0424 345 368; www.lentilasanything.com; 41 Blessington St, St Kilda; by donation; noon-9pm; ; 3, 16, 96)

Matcha Mylkbar

CAFE, VEGETARIAN $$

12 Map p142, B3

If you've spied anything from Matcha Mylkbar in your Instagram feed, it's likely you've been left green with envy. This small, contemporary St Kilda cafe is known for its matcha-heavy menu, which is also 100% plant based and vegan friendly. (03-9534 1111; www.matchamylkbar. com; 72a Acland St, St Kilda; dishes $15-22; 8am-3pm; ; 3, 16, 96)

Monk Bodhi Dharma

CAFE $

13 Map p142, E4

Monk Bodhi Dharma's location, down an alley off Carlisle St (next to Woolworths), means it doesn't get much foot traffic, which is lucky given that this cosy brick cafe has enough devotees as it is. A former 1920s bakehouse, it's now all about transcendental vegetarian food, from house-made bircher muesli to zucchini and mint hotcakes. House-roasted single-estate coffee tops things off.

 Local Life

Galleon Cafe

Affable and reassuringly worn, this '80s veteran **cafe** (03-9534 8934; 9 Carlisle St, St Kilda; mains from $10; 7am-5pm; 3, 16, 96) is a true St Kilda institution, having pumped caffeine, grub and Bloody Marys into generations of local writers, musos and eccentrics. Especially hectic at weekends, the cafe serves a decent choice of tasty, straightforward dishes, from French toast, porridge and pancakes to scrambled tofu and house-baked muffins and cakes.

Lentil as Anything

(☎03-9534 7250; rear 202 Carlisle St, Balaclava; dishes $9-19; ⏰7am-5pm Mon-Fri, from 8am Sat & Sun; 🖉; 🚊3, 16, 78)

Mr Wolf

PIZZA $$

15 ✖ Map p142, C3

Local celeb chef Karen Martini's casual but stylish space is renowned for its crisp Roman-style pizzas. There's also a great menu of antipasti and pastas that display her flair for matching ingredients. (☎03-9534 0255; www.mrwolf.com.au; 9-15 Inkerman St, St Kilda; pizza $20-25; ⏰5pm-late Tue-Sun, from noon Fri-Sun; 🚊3, 16, 67)

Si Señor

MEXICAN $

15 ✖ Map p142, E4

Si Señor is one of the most authentic Mexican joints in the city. Tasty spit-and-grilled meats are heaped onto soft corn tortillas under the direction of the place's Mexican owner. If you've overdone the hot sauce, cool it down with an authentic *horchata* (a delicious rice-milk and cinnamon drink). (☎03-9995 1083; www.sisenor. com.au; 193 Carlisle St, Balaclava; tacos $6-6.50, burritos $13-14.50; ⏰noon-3pm & 5-10pm Mon-Thu, noon-10pm Fri-Sun; 🖉; 🚊3, 16, 78, 🚉Balaclava)

Understand

Melbourne's Live-Music Scene

Melbourne's cultural image has involved music since producing two of the most enduringly fascinating talents of the 19th and early 20th centuries. Opera diva Dame Nellie Melba was an international star who lived overseas for many years but retained a sentimental attachment to her home town (hence the name). Percy Grainger, whose innovative compositions and performances prefigured many forms of 20th-centurymusic, was born and brought up in Melbourne. Grainger's eccentric genius extended beyond music to the design of clothing and objects; he was also known for his transgressive sex life. His life story is on display at the Grainger Museum (p129).

More recently, Melbourne's live-music scene exploded in the mid-1960s with a band called the Loved Ones, who broke the imitative mould of American '50s rock 'n' roll. The early 1970s saw groups such as AC/DC, Skyhooks and Daddy Cool capture the experience of ordinary Melbourne life in their lyrics for the first time. By the end of that decade, punk had descended. Nick Cave's Boys Next Door and the so-called 'Little Bands' shrieked their way through gigs at St Kilda's Crystal Ballroom (now the George Hotel). Bands and performers that grew out of (and beyond) this scene included the Birthday Party (evolving into Nick Cave and the Bad Seeds), the Models, Dead Can Dance, X, Primitive Calculators and the Moodists.The '80s pub-rock scene also gave birth to Crowded House, Paul Kelly, Hunters & Collectors and Australian Crawl, while the '90s and 2000s punk/grunge era saw the likes of the Cosmic Psychos, the Meanies, Powder Monkeys, Magic Dirt and Eddy Current Suppression Ring carry the torch passed on from their late-'70s predecessors. There's an ongoing threat of music venues being closed down due to noise complaints by some inner-city residents; sadly St Kilda's iconic pub, the Esplanade, is the latest victim and as of early 2017 its future as a live-music venue remains uncertain. Despite this, Melbourne still has a plethora of great venues spread throughout the city and inner suburbs and remains the live-music capital of Australia.

Drinking

Bar Di Stasio   WINE BAR

16 🚇 Map p142, B2

Within Pompidou-style scaffolding – the work of artist Callum Morton – lies this buzzing, grown-up bar, dominated by a floor-to-ceiling mural of Caravaggio's *Flagellation of Christ*. Behind the deep marble bar, waiters seemingly plucked from Venice's Caffè Florian mix perfect Campari *spritzes* while dishing out gorgeous bites, from lightly fried local seafood to elegant pastas (available until 11pm). Book: the place is extremely popular. (📞03-9525 3999; http://distasio.com.au/about/bar-di-stasio; 31 Fitzroy St, St Kilda; ⏱11.30am-midnight; 🚋3, 12. 16, 96)

Pontoon   BAR

Beneath the fine-dining Stokehouse (p145) is its casual, buzzing bar-bistro (see 9 🍴 Map p142, B3) , a light-soaked space with floor-to-ceiling windows and a deck looking right out at the beach and sunset. Slip on the shades and sip craft suds or a local prosecco while eyeing the crowd for the odd local celeb. A shared-plates menu delivers some decent bites, overpriced and undersized pizzas aside. (📞03-9525 5445; http://pontoonstkildabeach.com.au; 30 Jacka Blvd, St Kilda; ⏱noon-midnight; 🚋3, 16, 96)

Local Taphouse   BAR

17 🚇 Map p142, E3

Reminiscent of an old-school Brooklyn bar, the warm, wooden Local has a rotating cast of craft beers and an impressive bottle list. There's a beer garden upstairs, and a snug drawing-room mix of leather couches and open fires inside. Weekly events include live comedy (including well-established acts) on Monday, and live soul, funk, blues or reggae on Friday and Saturday. (📞03-9537 2633; www.thelocal.com.au; 184 Carlisle St, St Kilda; ⏱noon-late; 🚋3, 16, 78, 🚉Balaclava)

Republica   BAR

18 🚇 Map p142, A3

Opening right up to St Kilda Beach, Republica is about as close as you'll get to a beach bar in Melbourne. Ditch

---

🔵 Local Life
St Kilda Bowling Club

This fabulously intact old **clubhouse** (📞03-9534 5229; www.stkildasportsclub.com.au; 66 Fitzroy St, St Kilda; ⏱noon-late; 🚋12, 16, 96) is tucked behind a trimmed hedge and a splendid bowling green. The long bar serves drinks at 'club prices' (ie cheap) and you'll be joined by St Kilda's hippest on Sunday afternoons. Kick off your shoes, roll a few bowls, knock back beers and watch the sun go down along with your bowling accuracy.

the daytime food and head in later in the afternoon or in the evening for sunset beers, cocktail lounging and the odd flirtatious glance. (☏03-8598 9055; www.republica.net.au; St Kilda Sea Baths, 10-18 Jacka Blvd, St Kilda; ⊙11.30am-late Mon-Fri, from 9am Sat & Sun; 🛜; 🚌3, 16, 96)

Entertainment

Astor   CINEMA

19 ⭐ Map p142, E1

This 1936 art-deco darling has had more ups and downs than a Hollywood diva. Recently saved from permanent closure, it's one of Melbourne's best-loved landmarks, with double features most nights and a mixed bag of recent releases, art-house films and cult classics. Discount tickets ($12 to $13) are available Monday, Wednesday and Thursday. (☏03-9510 1414; www.astortheatre.net.au; cnr Chapel St & Dandenong Rd, Windsor; tickets $17; 🚌5, 64, 78, 🚃Windsor)

Prince Bandroom   LIVE MUSIC

20 ⭐ Map p142, B2

The Prince is a legendary St Kilda venue, with a solid line-up of local and international acts spanning hip-hop, dance, rock and indie. It's an eclectic mix, with recent guests including UK rapper Tinie Tempah, American roots-rock trio Moreland & Arbuckle and Nordic hardcore-punk outfit Refused. (☏03-9536 1168; www.princebandroom.com.au; 29 Fitzroy St, St Kilda; 🚌12, 16, 96)

Red Stitch Actors Theatre   THEATRE

21 ⭐ Map p142, E1

Featuring prolific national talent, Red Stitch is one of Australia's most respected actors' ensembles, staging new international works that are often premieres in Australia. The company's intimate black-box theatre is located opposite the historic Astor cinema, down the end of a driveway. (☏03-9533 8082; www.redstitch.net; rear 2 Chapel St, Windsor; 🚌5, 64, 78, 🚃Windsor)

Shopping

St Kilda Esplanade Market   MARKET

22 🔒 Map p142, A3

Fancy a Sunday stroll shopping by the seaside? Well, here's the place, with a kilometre of trestle tables joined end to end. Pick up anything from local ceramics, sculpture, glassware and woodwork to photographic prints, organic soaps and tongue-in-cheek, retro tea towels. (www.stkildaesplanademarket.com.au; Esplanade, St Kilda; ⊙10am-4pm Sun May-Sep, to 5pm Oct-Apr; 🚌3, 12, 16, 96)

Bitch is Back   DESIGN

23 🔒 Map p142, C3

This bitch offers a fabulous treasure trove of high-end vintage and mid-20th-century furniture and other design objects. There's an emphasis on Danish and Italian pieces from the

REBECCA SKINNER/GETTY IMAGES ©

Dot & Herbey

1920s to the 1980s, from armchairs and table lamps to glassware and ceramics. You might also stumble across highly sought-after furniture by European-trained, Australian-based designers like the Rosando Brothers, Dario Zoureff and Jakob Rudowski. (☏03-9534 8025; www.thebitchisback.com.au; 100a Barkly St, St Kilda; ⊘closed Mon; 🚋3, 16, 67)

Dot & Herbey FASHION & ACCESSORIES

24 🔒 Map p142, C4

Grandma Dot and Grandpa Herb smile down upon this tiny corner bou-tique from a mural-sized photo, right at home among the vintage floral fabrics, Japanese linen and understated bohemian cool. Scan the racks for grandpa tops, cotton overalls, beautiful knits and other pieces in gorgeous, ethical fabrics. (☏03-9593 6309; www.dotandherbey.com; 229 Barkly St, St Kilda; ⊘10.30am-6.30pm Mon-Wed, to 7pm Thu & Fri, 10am-6pm Sat & Sun; 🚋96)

The Best of
Melbourne

Melbourne's Best Walks

Melbourne's Best...

Melbourne CBD by night
TARAS VYSHNYA/SHUTTERSTOCK ©

Best Walks
A Seaside St Kilda Stroll

🏃 The Walk

With its palm-fringed promenades and long stretch of sand, St Kilda is made for wandering. It was once a playground full of dance halls, a fun park, theatres, sea baths and gardens. Despite a roller-coaster history of seediness and the more recent glitzy development, there are still remnants of the art deco mansions, and more than an air of the decadent heyday. This walk takes you through some of this seaside vibe.

Start St Kilda Pier; 🚋16, 96

Finish St Kilda Botanical Gardens; 🚋96

Length 3km; two hours

🍴 Take a Break

There's no better setting for coffee and cake than in the historic St Kilda Pier kiosk. You'll find plenty of cafes and restaurants along Acland St, but we recommend bypassing them until you hit Barkly St where you can feast on seafood at **Claypots** (p145).

Kiosk on St Kilda Pier

❶ St Kilda Pier & Kiosk

Stroll along historic **St Kilda Pier** (p141) for panoramic city and Port Phillip Bay views. The kiosk burnt down in 2003, just a year shy of its centenary, but was restored in 2006.

❷ St Kilda Beach

Keep walking onto famous St Kilda Beach. When summer hits, it packs out with locals and tourists looking for a patch of sand. While it may not be azure waters and white sands, for a city beach it's a winner.

❸ Pontoon

Along the beachfront, beneath the newly rebuilt, architecturally striking Stokehouse, you'll find stylish **Pontoon** (p149), perfect for a beverage on the deck overlooking Port Phillip Bay. Quench your thirst and soak up the ritzy atmosphere.

4 Linden New Art

Dust off the sand and head to the quiet end of Acland St to find **Linden New Art** (p144). The not-for-profit gallery is housed in a historical Victorian mansion and showcases contemporary works.

5 Palais Theatre

Further along the Esplanade, the **Palais Theatre** (p141) is one of the best examples of art deco in Melbourne. This former cinema has acted as a concert venue for many years hosting ballet, opera, and local and international bands.

6 Luna Park

Across the road you'll hear the screams from people hurtling on the historic roller-coaster at **Luna Park** (p141). Mr Moon has been swallowing people at the entrance since it opened in 1912. There's the usual whiplash-inducing rides and a beautiful baroque carousel.

7 Monarch Cake Shop

In business since 1934, the **Monarch** (p145) is one of the best Eastern European cake stores on the strip and is known for delicious *kugelhopf* (marble cake).

8 St Kilda Botanical Gardens

Escape the hustle in the backstreets off Acland St, where these **Gardens** (p144) remain a local favourite. Spread out a picnic blanket among indigenous plants and trees.

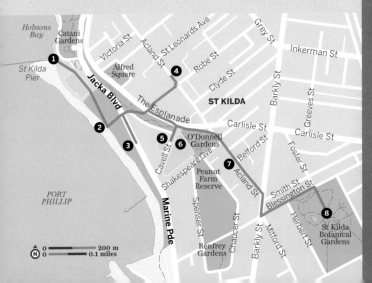

Best Walks
Classic City Melbourne

🏃 The Walk

If at first glance Melbourne seems thin on genuine world-class sights, your outlook will be swayed by a morning or afternoon absorbing the city's unique offerings. Melbourne has something for everyone's taste, from the grandeur of gold-rush-era buildings to green spaces, art galleries to graffiti-filled laneways, hip bars and trendy restaurants to markets and history.

Start 🚉 Flinders Street Station; Flinders St

Finish Queen Victoria Market; 🚋 9, 55, 57, 59

Length 3km; four hours

✗ Take a Break

For the quintessential Melbourne laneway dining experience, you can't beat tasty Spanish tapas at oh-so-cool **MoVida** (p40). For a more classic setting, duck into **Young & Jackson's** (p25) for coffee and cake, an upscale pub meal or a cold beer.

Old Treasury Building

❶ Federation Square

While its quirky design may have critics, **Federation Square** (p24) has become accepted as the city's gathering point. It's also home to the world-class Ian Potter Centre: NGV Australia art gallery and Australian Centre for the Moving Image.

❷ Birrarung Marr

An oasis in the heart of the city, **Birrarung Marr** (p26) offers a peaceful stroll alongside the Yarra River through indigenous vegetation, and Aboriginal installations and sculptures. It's a scenic place for a BBQ by the river, and provides fantastic photo ops.

❸ Hosier Lane

In a city famed for street art, **Hosier Lane** (p34) is ground zero, attracting everyone from graffiti artists to curious photo-snapping locals and tourists. Expect graffiti, stencils, murals and paste-ups.

JOHN ABBATE/SHUTTERSTOCK ©

4 Old Treasury Building

Wind your way up Flinders Lane and Collins St to this stately 19th-century Renaissance Revival–style **building** (p36). Today a museum, its grandeur is symbolic of the wealth of the gold-rush boom years in the 1850s.

5 Chinatown

This strip of Chinese (and other Asian) restaurants is a legacy from the influx of Chinese gold-rush settlers in the1850s. Put it into context by visiting the **Chinese Museum** (p34).

6 State Library of Victoria

Duck into this stunning **library** (p36) to learn why Melbourne is recognised by Unesco as a City of Literature. It houses more than two million books, a stunning reading room, fantastic exhibits and Ned Kelly's armour.

7 Old Melbourne Gaol

It may have closed its doors in 1929, but this bluestone **prison** (p36) remains as grim as ever. It's one of Melbourne's most popular museums. Tour the cells and learn about the executions of notorious inmates such as Ned Kelly.

8 Queen Victoria Market

This 19th-century **market** (p28) is a great place to buy fresh produce, gourmet foods and Australiana souvenirs.

Best
Eating

Melbourne's reputation as a culinary destination has been shaped significantly by its history of migration. Greeks, Italians, Lebanese, Indians, Chinese, Vietnamese and people from many other ethnicities have all left their mark, and Melbourne's best contemporary restaurants gainfully plunder them all. Melburnians are adventurous in their dining habits, and the best places are never secrets for long.

Dishing up Diversity

Take 140 cultures, mix and let simmer for a few decades. While the recipe might not be quite that simple, Victoria's culinary habits are truly multicultural. Many Melburnians have grown up with at least one other culinary heritage besides the rather grim Anglo-Australian fare of the mid-20th century, and they are also inveterate travellers. This makes for a city of adventurous palates.

Eating Local

Queen Victoria Market in Melbourne's city centre, and its suburban counterparts in South Melbourne and Prahran, are beloved by locals for their fresh fruit, vegetables, meat and fish, and their groaning deli counters. There's also a weekly rota of inner-city farmers markets (see www.mfm.com.au) at Collingwood Children's Farm and South Melbourne's Gasworks, which bring local artisan producers and fresh, often organic, produce to town. A highlight is the Slow Food Farmers' Market held at Abbotsford Convent.

Food Trucks

Melbourne's long had an association with food vans; a game of suburban footy isn't complete without someone dishing out hot jam doughnuts, hot meat pies and hot chips to freezing fans over a truck counter. But getting quality food from a van is a different matter. Taking a cue from LA's food-truck revolution, fabulous options have begun plying the streets of Melbourne in recent years. Each day the trucks post to let their Twitter and Facebook followers know where they'll be, and hungry folk dutifully respond by turning up street-side for a meal.

Best Cafe Fare

St Ali Try the corn fritters at this South Melbourne institution. (p68)

Proud Mary The food here is just as good as the excellent coffee. (p112)

Best Vegetarian

Smith & Deli Vegan deli fare, including some surprisingly convincing fake meat. (p108)

Lentil as Anything Long-time favourite, with branches in St Kilda and Abbotsford. (p146)

Monk Bodhi Dharma Healthy food and great coffee. (p146)

Best Budget Eats

Hakata Gensuke Queues perpetually stretch out the door for Melbourne's best ramen. (p38)

St Ali The consummate Melbourne cafe. (p68)

Smith & Deli A vegan take on a New York deli deep in the heart of Fitzroy. (p108)

Thy Thy Cheap and cheerful Vietnamese in a local Richmond favourite. (p94)

Best Splurge

Attica Modern Australian cuisine at its best. (p144)

Lee Ho Fook Fabulously fun and riotously tasty take on Chinese cooking. (p37)

Cutler & Co Intimate contemporary Australian restaurant, in Fitzroy. (p108)

Woodland House Modern Australian in a beautiful villa. (p80)

Best Local & Indigenous Cuisine

Charcoal Lane Try native ingredients such as wattleseed and finger lime. (p109)

Vue de Monde The best of Australian ingredients with stunning views. (p38)

Best Seafood

Stokehouse Modern seafood dishes by the bay. (p145)

Rockpool Bar & Grill Fill up at the seafood raw bar. (p54)

Claypots Pots full of fresh seafood. (p145)

Best Sweets

Zumbo (p80)

Pidapipo (p132)

Jock's Ice-Cream (p69)

Gelato Messina (p108)

Brunetti (p132)

Best
Parks & Gardens

If Victoria is the garden state, then Melbourne is the garden city. You'll enjoy an abundance of green spaces dotted around town. Whether you're checking out native species in the botanical gardens, admiring 19th-century heritage gardens or picnicking like a local in inner-city green spaces, you'll never be short of a leafy refuge.

GREG BRAVE/SHUTTERSTOCK ©

Best Inner-City Green Space

Birrarung Marr Wander through the grassy knolls, river promenades and thoughtful planting of indigenous flora at this city park – complete with great viewpoints of the city and river. (p26)

Fitzroy Gardens On the fringe of the central business district (CBD), you'll find sprawling lawns and grand avenues; also home to Cooks' Cottage (shipped brick by brick from England). (p93)

Herring Island On an island in the middle of the Yarra you can see the original trees and grasses of the Yarra, It's also home to an impressive environmental sculpture collection. (p79)

Best Botanical Gardens

Royal Botanic Gardens Up there with the best botanical gardens in the world, with herb gardens and an indigenous rainforest. (p74)

St Kilda Botanical Gardens A hidden gem in St Kilda's quiet backstreets, where you can laze around with a good book like a local. (p144)

Best
With Kids

Best Parks & Gardens

Birrarung Marr Within this green space, ArtPlay runs fun creative workshops. (p26)

Ian Potter Foundation Children's Garden Interactive garden where kids can discover the natural world. (p75)

Fitzroy Gardens Explore Cooks' Cottage and the Fairies Tree. (p93)

Best Museums

Melbourne Museum A 3D volcano, a living forest and state-of-the-art displays of Indigenous storytelling. (p122)

Scienceworks Entertaining and educational, with plenty of crazy experiments to carry out. (p61)

Old Melbourne Gaol

Educational and memorable for kids over 10 who can explore the historic jail cells. (p36)

National Sports Museum Sporty sprogs of any age can test their skills shooting hoops, kicking goals and cycle sprinting. (p91)

Best Outdoors

St Kilda Foreshore Build sand castles and splash in the bay on summer days. (p140)

Luna Park With bumper cars and roller-coasters, this amusement park guarantees fun. (p141)

Best Animal Encounters

Collingwood Children's Farm Inner-city farm with loads of frolicking animals. (p119)

VEVCHIC/SHUTTERSTOCK ©

Melbourne Zoo Australia's oldest zoo with a large number of native animals. (p128)

Best Rainy-Day Activities

ACMI Have a go at sound editing and film yourself in a Matrix-style slow-motion stop-frame sequence. (p25)

State Library of Victoria Check out Ned Kelly's armour. (p36)

Best
Drinking &
Nightlife

Melbourne's drinking scene is easily the best in Australia and as good as any in the world. There's a huge diversity of venues, ranging from hip basement dives hidden down laneways to sophisticated cocktail bars perched on rooftops. Many pubs have pulled up the beer-stained carpet and polished the concrete, but don't dismiss the character-filled oldies that still exist.

JODIE JOHNSON/SHUTTERSTOCK ©

Craft Beer & Microbreweries

Until recently, thirsty Melburnians were given the choice of only two or three mainstream beers on tap (and perhaps an interstate lager if they were feeling adventurous). But the last decade has seen the emergence of microbreweries and craft-beer bars, primed to meet the demands of beer geeks who treat their drinking more seriously.

Coffee Culture

Melbourne's coffee tradition stems back to the arrival of Italian immigrants, but these days it's not just a shot of strong espresso on the menu. Direct-trade single origin beans and speciality brews such as siphon, pour over and cold drip are *de rigueur*. There's a reason Melbourne's coffee is so celebrated: much of it is roasted here.

Best Microbreweries & Craft Beer Bars

Mountain Goat Brewery Occupies a large warehouse in Richmond's backstreets; drop by for tours, tasting paddles and pizza. (p98)

Stomping Ground Brewery & Beer Hall Set in a former textile factory. (p113)

Local Taphouse One of St Kilda's finest establishments for craft beer. (p149)

Best Rooftop Bars

Naked for Satan An unbeatable roof terrace in Fitzroy with a wraparound decked balcony. (p112)

Madame Brussels Camp fun, with a kooky tennis-club vibe. (p42)

Rooftop Bar, Curtain House

Rooftop Bar Curtin House is so replete with cool venues that they even spill out onto the roof. (p43)

Siglo Gaze over Parliament House and St Pat's from this upmarket eyrie. (p42)

Best Cocktail Bars

Lui Bar Try the signature macadamia martini and gaze out at the city (p44)

Bar Americano Expertly made cocktails. (p42)

Everleigh Sophisticated 'golden era' cocktails in a hidden upstairs Fitzroy bar. (p112)

Black Pearl Award-winning cocktails on Brunswick St, Fitzroy. (p112)

Rufus All chandeliers and champagne cocktails in Prahran. (p82)

Best Music Bars & Pubs

The Tote Divey Collingwood pub that's one of the city's most loved live-music venues. (p114)

Cherry Things get noisy at this dark-walled venue on AC/DC Lane (where else?). (p31)

Corner Mid-sized venue for international bands and the more successful locals. (p98)

Yellow Bird Owned by a local musician; knock back drinks to a great soundtrack. (p84)

Heartbreaker Nothing but great rock and punk tunes in this central city bar. (p42)

Best Coffee

Market Lane Try an on-site roasted coffee as you peruse the Prahran Market. (p82)

Seven Seeds Hidden away warehouse cafe with superb coffee. (p133)

Proud Mary Serious coffee specialists in Collingwood. (p112)

Padre Coffee Premium single-origin brews in East Brunswick. (p101)

Industry Beans Helpful staff will guide you at this coffee chemistry cafe. (p113)

Best Laneway Bars

Bar Americano Standing room only at this superb city cocktail bar. (p42)

Cherry Legendary divey rock bar tucked down AC/DC Lane. (p31)

Croft Institute It's a science in itself just finding this lab-themed bar. (p42)

Best
For Free

Melbourne may be at the higher end of the price scale but there is a decent choice of free offerings in the city. Whether it's gallery-hopping or checking out street art and museums, there are plenty of ways to save those pennies.

NEALE COUSLAND/SHUTTERSTOCK ©

Best Museums & Art

Ian Potter Centre: NGV Australia Check out the excellent permanent collection of Australian art. (p34)

NGV International Expansive permanent collection of international art including Rembrandt, Bacon and Picasso. (p50)

Hosier Lane Best known street-art laneway in the city. (p34)

Australian Centre for Contemporary Art Challenging contemporary art museum exhibiting local and international works. (p53)

Australian Centre for the Moving Image Well-curated collection of interactive exhibits relating to Australian TV and cinema. (p25)

Best Sights & Activities

Federation Square Learn about the city's prominent architectural square on a guided tour. (p24)

Birrarung Marr City park featuring indigenous flora, Aboriginal art and sculptures. (p26)

City Circle Tram Take a scenic ride through the city on a historic tram. (p36)

State Library of Victoria Admire the stunning La Trobe Reading Room and check out Ned Kelly's armour. (p36)

Shrine of Remembrance Take a guided tour of this war memorial with a returned soldier. (p78)

NEALE COUSLAND/SHUTTERSTOCK ©

Best Indigenous Culture

While the Indigenous Wurundjeri people have inhabited Melbourne for around 50,000 years, sadly they make up a minute percentage of the population. Thankfully, however, in recent years there have been strong efforts to educate about and promote Wurundjeri culture and way of life through walking tours, artwork, or Indigenous-inspired cuisine. There are also museums detailing the devastation and hardships encountered with the arrival of European settlers.

Melbourne Museum Features the Bunjilaka Aboriginal Cultural Centre. (p122)

Ian Potter Centre: NGV Australia Extraordinarily beautiful collection of Aboriginal art. (p34)

Birrarung Marr City parkland incorporating Indigenous themes including art installations and stories of Wurundjeri people. (p26)

Charcoal Lane Restaurant showcasing Indigenous flavours. (p109)

Koorie Heritage Trust A mix of an Indigenous museum, gallery and shop with tours of Flagstaff Gardens. (p35)

Aboriginal Heritage Walk Learn how the Wurundjeri lived on this walking tour through the Botanic Gardens. (p74)

State Library of Victoria Features exhibits that delve into the Wurundjeri's first encounters with colonial settlers and a controversial treaty signed with John Batman. (p36)

Melbourne Cricket Ground Aussie Rules footy is an Indigenous game, and the surrounding MCG parkland is home to scar trees. (p94)

Best
Shopping

Melbourne is a city of passionate, dedicated retailers. It's particularly good for small, independent clothing boutiques as well as a number of great markets for art and design, along with gourmet goods. From city laneways and arcades to suburban shopping streets and malls, you'll find plenty of places to loosen your wallet and pick up something unique.

City Centre

The city has national and international chains spread out over Bourke, Swanston and Collins Sts, as well as the city malls of Melbourne Central and QV. Smaller retailers and design workshops inhabit the laneways as well as the vertical villages of Curtin House and the Nicholas Building. Flinders Lane and the arcades and laneways that feed into it are particularly blessed. A strip of Little Collins heading east from Swanston is dedicated to sartorially savvy gentlemen, while the length of leafy Collins St is lined with luxury retailers.

Neighbourhoods

Chapel St, South Yarra, has all the chains and classic Australian names, as well as some edgier designers once you hit Prahran. You'll find streetwear in Greville St, Prahran, and in Windsor; the latter is also good for vintage shopping. Brunswick St,

Fitzroy, has streetwear and vintage shops, and pulses with the energy of young designers. Gertrude St, Fitzroy, mixes vintage with many of the city's most sought-after innovators, as well as some up-and-coming menswear names, art-supply shops and vintage furniture.

Melbourne Black

One constant in Melbourne fashion is colour, or lack of it. You'll not go long without hearing mention of 'Melbourne black', and it's true that inky shades are worn not just during the cold months but right through the hottest days of summer. Perhaps it's because black somehow suits the soft light and often grey days, or maybe it's the subliminal influence of the city's moody bluestone. Some muse that it's the long-lingering fallout of the explosive 1980s post-punk scene or southern European immigration. The fact remains that black clothes sell far better here than in any other

Best Fashion

Scanlan Theodore
Men's and women's clothing by a mix of Scandinavian and local designers. (p87)

Alpha60 The gorgeous chapter-house branch of this local women's label is retail at its finest. (p46)

Dot & Herbey Cute women's boutique in St Kilda. (p151)

Best Bookstores

Readings Local favourite indie bookstore with a great selection. (p136)

Brunswick Street Bookstore Beloved local spot in the heart of Brunswick Street. (p117)

Avenue Books Great staff and lovely Albert Park village location. (p70)

Best Markets

Rose Street Artists' Market Great for art and crafts. (p116)

St Kilda Esplanade Market Everything from ceramics and glassware to organic soaps and retro tea towels. (p150)

Best Food Shopping

Queen Victoria Market The city's bustling open-air market crammed with gourmet delights and local flavours. (p28)

South Melbourne Market Great for fresh local produce and deli items. (p66)

Prahran Market Stuffed with produce and has its own cooking school. (p81)

Gewürzhaus Stop in for a range of spices. (p136)

Best Art & Design

Craft Victoria Showcases handmade goods by local artisans. (p46)

ArtBoy Gallery Local art that's edgy and unique, and surprisingly affordable. (p85)

Third Drawer Down Kooky objects and high-end art. (p116)

Mud Australia Beautiful Australian-made ceramics. (p116)

Best Music Stores

Basement Discs City centre location in an arcade. (p46)

Greville Records Prahran institution with excellent vinyl collection. (p86)

Polyester Records A love for local bands and knowledgeable staff. (p116)

Worth a Trip

Filled with secondhand and handcrafted goods, **Camberwell Sunday Market** (www.camberwellsundaymarket.org; Market Pl; ⊙6.30am-12.30pm Sun; ⊠Camberwell) is where Melburnians come to offload their unwanted items and where antique hunters come to find them. It's great for discovering preloved (often rarely worn) items of clothing, restocking a bookcase and finding unusual curios.

Best
Live
Entertainment

Whether it's ball games or ballet that gets your pulse racing, Melbourne's very full calendar is bound to have something for you. The city likes to think of itself as both the sporting and the cultural capital of Australia – an odd mix, perhaps, but one that's widely embraced by locals.

JE JIM/SHUTTERSTOCK ©

Live Music

There's a constant procession of big international acts hitting local stadiums, arenas and theatres, and many of Melbourne's smaller drinking dens and pubs double as live-music venues. Check daily papers and street magazines Beat (www.beat.com.au) and The Music (www.themusic.com.au) for gig info. Radio station 3RRR (102.7FM; www.rrr.org.au) broadcasts a gig guide at 7pm from Wednesday to Friday, and at 6pm on weekends.

Opera

Melbourne has nurtured internationally acclaimed opera singers and continues to stage world-class productions. People do dress up for a night at the opera, especially Opera Australia's opening and weekend nights, but no one will raise an eyebrow if you don't.

Theatre

Melbourne's longstanding theatrical heritage is evident in the city's legacy of Victorian-era theatres, such as the Princess and Athenæum. While the blockbusters pack out these grand dames, Melbourne's theatre scene encompasses a wide spectrum of genres. The most high-profile company is the Melbourne Theatre Company (MTC; www.mtc.com.au), which stages performances year-round.

Sport

Melbourne is a sport-obsessed city. From March to October it's all about AFL footy, while rugby league, rugby union and the other kind of football (ie soccer) are also very popular. In summer, cricket dominates.

Arts Centre Melbourne

Best Live Music

The Tote Divey Collingwood pub that's one of the city's most loved live-music venues. (p114)

Cherry Melbourne's legendary live-rock bar on AC/DC Lane. (p31)

Corner Midsized venue for international bands and the more successful locals. (p98)

Best Theatre Companies

Melbourne Theatre Company The big one, staging works in its own excellent Southbank Theatre. (p56)

Malthouse Theatre Exciting company

dedicated to staging contemporary Australian plays. (p58)

La Mama The mother of independent theatre in Melbourne. (p135)

Best Classical Music, Opera & Dance

Arts Centre Melbourne The city's most prominent conglomeration of concert halls and theatres. (p53)

Melbourne Recital Centre Modern venue with extraordinary acoustics. (p57)

Melbourne Opera Not-for-profit company that performs classic and

light opera in various venues. (p45)

Chunky Move An acclaimed contemporary-dance company that performs mainly at the Malthouse Theatre. (p58)

Sporting Venues

Melbourne Park Home of the Australian Open tennis championships. (p98)

MCG Sacred ground for AFL footy and cricket matches. (p90)

Albert Park Lake Circuit for the Australian Formula One Grand Prix. (p67)

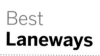

Best
Laneways

Nothing screams Melbourne quite as loudly as a graffiti-covered lane – preferably one hiding a cafe, basement bar or sought-after restaurant. The most famous (and most photographed) of them all is Hosier Lane, with little Rutledge Lane jutting off it like a separate wing of the same gallery. There are plenty of other such street-art-bedecked stretches to sniff out (some of them are genuinely whiffy) all around the central city.

Best Laneway Bars

Croft Institute Cool hidden bar in a street-art-splashed laneway. (p42)

Bar Americano Standing-room only for excellent cocktails. (p42)

Best Laneway Cafes

Degraves Espresso In bustling Degraves St; does a roaring trade. (p31)

Best Laneways Restaurants

Lee Ho Fook Modern Chinese in gritty laneway. (p37)

Tonka Located at the end of a skungy laneway but all elegance inside. (p40)

MoVida Spanish tapas in the city's best-known lane for street art. (p40)

Coda Basement and city laneway setting for all the more cool cred. (p38)

Best Street Art

Hosier Lane Melbourne's street art mecca. (p34)

Melbourne Street Tours Walking tours by street artists. (p34)

Artists Lane Bluestone laneway covered in art in Windsor. (p86)

MELANIE CONROY/500PX ©

Best
Gay & Lesbian

QUINN ROONEY/GETTY IMAGES ©

Melbourne has a large gay and lesbian population, second in Australia only to Sydney, and it's generally a very accepting city. Although same-sex marriage isn't legal, there's equality in most other aspects of the law. While there's still a handful of specifically gay venues scattered around the city, some of the best hangouts are weekly takeovers of mainstream bars. The two best areas for finding the best venues are in Abbotsford and Collingwood in the inner north, and Prahran and South Yarra in the inner south.

Festivals & Events

The big event on the queer calendar is the annual **Midsumma Festival** (www.midsumma. org.au; ⊙ Jan/Feb). It has a diverse program of cultural, community and sporting events, including the popular Midsumma Carnival at Alexandra Gardens, St Kilda's Pride March and much more. Australia's largest GLBT film festival, the **Melbourne Queer Film Festival** (www.melbournequeerfilm. com.au; ⊙ Mar), screens more than 100 films from around the world.

Resources

For more local info, pick up a copy of the free magazines Star Observer (www.starobserver.com.au), MCV (www.gaynews network.com.au) and LOTL (Lesbians on the Loose; www.lotl.com). Gay and lesbian radio station JOY 94.9FM (www.joy.org.au) is another important resource for visitors and locals.

Best Nightlife

Sircuit Hugely popular old-school gay bar with pool tables, a back room and a heaving dance floor. (p113)

Peel Hotel One of Melbourne's best-known gay venues; a reliable spot for a late-night boogie. (p114)

Laird A well established men-only pub complete with lots of leather and beer. (p113)

DT's Hotel An intimate gay pub hosting drag shows, karaoke, pool competitions and happy hours. (p97)

Best
Arts

Long regarded as the culture capital of Australia, Melbourne has always been a city for artists and art lovers. Its thriving live-music scene, strong community of street artists, and passion for literature, theatre and visual arts all provide a vibrant, creative backdrop fundamental to the fabric of the city. Art in Melbourne is highly accessible, in terms of the number of its art spaces and its appeal to a broad audience.

Visual Arts

Melbourne's visual-arts scene thrives and grows in myriad places: tucked away in basement galleries, exhibited in edgy spaces, stencilled on unmarked laneway walls, flaunted in world-class museums and sneaking up on you in parks and gardens.

Contemporary Art

Between the commercial, public and artist-run galleries, there is much to discover in Melbourne's contemporary arts scene. A good place to tap into it is Gertrude Contemporary Art Space, which hosts exhibitions by emerging artists and fosters innovative new works. The Australian

Centre for Contemporary Art (ACCA) also hosts cutting-edge exhibitions as well as developing large-scale projects. The Australian Centre for the Moving Image (ACMI) exhibits film and multimedia works by contemporary artists, and the Centre for Contemporary Photography has a strong photo- and film-based program.

Street Art

With its growing reputation for street art, Melbourne's urban landscape is a beacon for visitors from all around the world. Dozens of laneway walls provide an outdoor canvas for paste-up, mural and stencil art.

Heide Museum of Modern Art

Best Contemporary Art

Australian Centre for Contemporary Art
Showcases local and international artists. (p53)

Gertrude Contemporary Art Space
Highly reputable not-for-profit. (p107)

Best Australian Art Collections

Ian Potter Centre: NGV Australia
Great collection of Australian and Indigenous art (p34)

Alcaston Gallery
Focus on Indigenous art and works directly with communities. (p107)

Best International Art

NGV International
Hosts blockbuster shows by major names. (p50)

Justin House Art Museum
Private tour of the collection in an architecturally designed house. (p78)

Worth a Trip

Heide (✆9850 1500; www.heide.com. au; 7 Templestowe Rd, Bulleen; adult/ child $22/18; ⏱10am-5pm Tue-Sun; 🚌903 🚉Heidelberg) is a prestigious not-for-profit art gallery with a sculpture garden in its wonderful grounds and regularly changing exhibitions. The collection is spread over three buildings: a large purpose-built gallery, the Reeds' original farmhouse and the wonderful modernist house they built in 1963 as 'a gallery to be lived in'.

Best
Tours & Activities

Best Walking Tours

Walk-to-Art (☎0412 005 901; www.walktoart.com. au; 2/4hr tour $78/108) These walking tours take you to galleries and artist-run spaces hidden in buildings and laneways around the city centre and inner neighbourhoods. The longer tours depart at 2pm on Saturday, and there are express tours on Monday and Friday, and twilight tours at 6pm on Thursday.

Hidden Secrets Tours (☎9663 3358; www.hidden secretstours.com; tours from $29) Offers a variety of walking tours covering subjects such as lanes and arcades, history, architecture and cafe culture.

Melbourne By Foot (☎1300 311 081; www.mel bournebyfoot.com; departs Federation Sq; tours $40; ◷1pm; ☒Flinders St) Take a few hours out and experience a mellow, informative three-hour walking tour that covers laneway art, politics, Melbourne's history and diversity. Highly recommended; book online. There's also a Beer Lovers tour ($85).

Best Scenic

Kayak Melbourne Offers a variety of different tours, such as the 2½-hour Moonlight tour (from Docklands) or the ninety-minute City Sights tour paddling past Southbank to Docklands. (p53)

Global Ballooning (☎9428 5703; www. globalballooning.com.au; adult/child from $440/340) Wake up at the crack of dawn to view the city from another angle on this one-hour ride.

SUNFLOWEREY/SHUTTERSTOCK ©

Best Water Sports

Kite Republic (☎9537 0644; www.kiterepublic. com.au; St Kilda Sea Baths, 4/10-18 Jacka Blvd; 1hr lesson $90; ◷10am-6pm Mon-Fri, to 5pm Sat & Sun; ☒96) Offers kiteboarding lessons, tours and equipment; also a good source of info. In winter it can arrange snowkiting at Mt Hotham. Also rents stand-up paddleboards (SUPs) and street SUPs.

Stand Up Paddle HQ (☎0416 184 994; www. supb.com.au; St Kilda Pier; hire per hr $30, 1½hr tour $99; ☒96) Arrange a lesson or hire SUP equipment from St Kilda Pier, or consider joining its Yarra River tour.)

Survival Guide

Survival Guide

Before You Go

When to Go

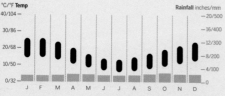

°C/°F **Temp**
40/104 —
30/86 —
20/68 —
10/50 —
0/32 —

J F M A M J J A S O N D

Rainfall inches/mm
— 20/500
— 16/400
— 12/300
— 8/200
— 4/100
— 0

➡ **Summer (Dec–Feb)**
Brings balmy nights, grand-slam tennis, cricket, music festivals and plenty of events.

➡ **Autumn (Mar–May)**
The Australian Formula One Grand Prix rolls into town and the Moomba festival takes over the weather. April arguably has the best weather.

➡ **Winter (Jun–Aug)**
Escape the cold with gallery-hopping, and toasty live-music venues. Grab your thermos and get rugged up at the footy.

➡ **Spring (Sep–Nov)**
Footy-finals fever hits before the horses start cantering in the lead-up to the Melbourne Cup.

Book Your Stay

➡ Prices peak during the Australian Open in January, Grand Prix weekend in March, AFL footy finals in September and the Spring Racing Carnival in November.

➡ Midrange to deluxe hotels publish 'rack rates', but you should always ask for current specials.

➡ In addition to the usual chains, there are some excellent boutique choices, from art-themed hotels to 19th-century splendour and rock 'n' roll chic.

➡ Stylish, self-contained apartment-style rooms are increasingly common in the central business district (CBD) and inner city, and provide excellent value.

➡ There's an abundance of hostels in Melbourne, from generic backpackers to more character-filled places in historical buildings and well-equipped flashpackers.

Useful Websites

Visit Victoria (www.visitvictoria.com) Official state tourist site, with accommodation listings.

Bed & Breakfast (www.bedandbreakfast.com.au) Lists more than 40 B&Bs scattered all over the city.

Lonely Planet (www.lonelyplanet.com/melbourne) Recommendations and bookings.

Best Budget

Nunnery (www.nunnery.com.au) Channel your inner sister, or not, at this former Fitzroy convent.

Melbourne Central YHA (www.yha.com.au) A slick, professional hostel with some great private rooms on the rooftop.

Best Midrange

Treasury on Collins (www.treasuryoncollins.com.au) As good as any top hotel but at better prices – and with free Netflix!

Tyrian Serviced Apartments (www.tyrian.com.au) Live like a Fitzroy local in this complex on the Johnston St strip.

Alto Hotel on Bourke (www.altohotel.com.au) Eco-conscious and handy to Southern Cross station.

Best Top End

Ovolo Laneways (www.ovolohotels.com.au) Hipster chic meets executive comfort in this city-centre boutique hotel.

QT Melbourne (www.qtmelbourne.com.au) Super-cool decor and a fabulous rooftop bar.

Adelphi Hotel (www.adelphi.com.au) Design-driven city-centre hotel in the hippest part of Flinders Lane.

Arriving in Melbourne

Melbourne Airport

Melbourne Airport (MEL; ☎03-9297 1600; www.melbourneairport.com.au; Departure Rd, Tullamarine) is the city's only international and main domestic airport, located 22km northwest of the city centre in Tullamarine.

➡ **SkyBus** (☎1300 759 287; www.skybus.com.au; Southern Cross station, 99 Spencer St; adult/child $18/9; ⛉Southern Cross) departs regularly and connects the airport to Southern Cross station 24 hours a day. There are also services to other parts of Melbourne, including St Kilda.

➡ The fare for a taxi to the city centre will start at around $55 and could hit $75 (including surcharges and tolls), depending on traffic and time of day.

Avalon Airport

Avalon Airport (☎03-5227 9100; www.avalonairport.com.au; 80 Beach Rd, Lara) Jetstar flies to and from Sydney, Gold Coast, Adelaide and Hobart. The airport is around 55km southwest of Melbourne's city centre.

SkyBus (☎03-9689 7999; www.skybus.com.au; adult/child $22/10) offers a direct bus service between Avalon and Melbourne's Southern Cross station.

Southern Cross Station

Southern Cross Station (☎03-9670 2072; www.travellersaid.org.au; Southern Cross station, 99 Spencer St; ⏱6.30am-9.30pm) Long-distance trains and buses arrive at this large station on the Docklands side of the city centre. From here it's easy to connect to metropolitan trains, buses and trams.

Great Southern Rail (☎1800 703 357; www.greatsouthernrail.com.au) Runs the *Overland* train between Melbourne and Adelaide.

V/Line (☎1800 800 007; www.vline.com.au) Operates the Victorian train and bus networks.

Firefly (☎1300 730 740; www.fireflyexpress.com.au; Southern Cross station, 99 Spencer St) Overnight buses to/from Sydney and Adelaide twice per week.

Greyhound (☎1300 473 946; www.greyhound.com.au) Buses Australia-wide.

Getting Around

Tram

➡ So very Melbourne, the city's trams crisscross the city centre and extend through much of the surrounding suburbs.

➡ Trams run roughly every 10 minutes during the day (more frequently in peak periods), and every 20 minutes in the evening.

➡ They run roughly every 10 minutes Monday to Friday, every 15 minutes on Saturday and every 20 minutes on Sunday.

➡ Trams run until midnight Sunday to Thursday, 1am Friday and Saturday, and six lines run all night on weekends.

Train

➡ Flinders Street Station is the main city hub. Many lines spin around the City Loop, which connects the five stations in the inner city (Flinders St, Southern Cross, Flagstaff, Melbourne Central and Parliament), before heading out again.

➡ Trains run from around 5am to around 11.30pm daily, and there is an all-night service to/from Flinders Street Station for most lines on Friday and Saturday nights.

Bus

➡ Melbourne has an extensive bus network, with over 300 routes covering all the places that the trains and trams don't go.

➡ Most routes run from 6am to 9pm weekdays, 8am to 9pm Saturdays and 9am to 9pm Sundays. Night Bus services operate after midnight on weekends to many suburbs.

➡ Night Bus services operate after midnight on weekends to many suburbs.

➡ **Melbourne Visitor Shuttle** (https://whatson.melbourne.vic.gov.au; 2 days $10; ⏱9.30am-3.45pm) is a hop-on, hop-off bus tour with an audio commentary, stopping at 13 of Melbourne's main sights on a 90-minute loop.

Bicycle

➡ Cycling maps and information are available from the **Melbourne**

Visitor Centre (☎03-9658 9658; https://whatson.melbourne.vic.gov.au; Federation Sq; ⏰9am-6pm; 📶; 🚇Flinders St) and **Bicycle Network** (☎03-8376 8888; www.bv.com.au).

➡ Helmets are compulsory.

➡ Conventional bikes can be taken on trains (but not the first carriage), but only folding bikes are allowed on trams or buses.

➡ **Melbourne Bike Share** (☎1300 711 590; www.melbournebikeshare.com.au; subscription day/week $3/8) is an automated, self-service bike-share system; look out for the 52 bright-blue stations scattered around the city, central suburbs and St Kilda. Some but not all bikes have safety helmets left with them; otherwise helmets are available with a $5 subsidy from 7-Eleven, IGA and bike stores around the city.

➡ For bike hire, try **Humble Vintage** (☎0424 619 262; www.thehumblevintage.com; 2hr/day/week $25/35/90) or **Rentabike** (☎0417 339 203; www.rentabike.net.au; Federation Wharf; rental per hr/day $15/40, 4hr tour incl lunch adult/child $110/79; ⏰10am-5pm; 🚇Flinders St).

Car & Motorcycle

Most car and campervan hire places have offices at Melbourne Airport and in the city or central suburbs:

Avis (☎03-8855 5333; www.avis.com.au)

Budget (☎1300 362 848; www.budget.com.au)

Europcar (☎1300 131 390; www.europcar.com.au)

Hertz (☎03-9663 6244; www.hertz.com.au)

Rent a Bomb (☎03-9428 0088; www.rentabomb.com.au; 452 Bridge Rd, Richmond; 🚌48, 75)

Thrifty (☎1300 367 227; www.thrifty.com.au)

➡ Where the trams run along the centre of the road, drivers cannot pass them once they indicate that they're

Tickets & Passes

Melbourne's buses, trams and trains use myki, a 'touch on, touch off' travel-pass system. It's not particularly convenient for short-term visitors as it requires you to purchase a $6 plastic myki card and then put credit on it before you travel.

➡ The myki can be topped up at 7-Eleven stores, machines at most train stations and at some tram stops in the city centre; online top-ups can take some time to process.

➡ For travel within metropolitan Melbourne (zones 1 and 2), the pay-as-you-go fare is $4.10 for two hours, or capped at $8.20 for the day ($6 on weekends).

➡ There are fines for travelling without having touched on a valid myki card; ticket inspectors are vigilant and unforgiving.

➡ For more information, see **PTV** (Public Transport Victoria; ☎1800 800 007; www.ptv.vic.gov.au).

stopping, as passengers board and alight from the street.

➡ In the city centre many intersections are marked 'right turn from left only'. This is the counter-intuitive 'hook turn', devised so as not to block trams or other cars.

➡ Car-sharing companies rent out cars by the hour(from $9) or the day (from $55) and prices include petrol. Companies vary in terms of joining fees ($12 to $70) and how they charge (insurance fees, per hour and per kilometre). The cars are parked in and around the city centre and inner suburbs in designated 'car share' spots. Some companies operating in Melbourne include:

Flexi Car (☑1300 363 780; www.flexicar.com.au).

Go Get (☑1300 769 389; www.goget.com.au)

Green Share Car (☑1300 575 878; www. greensharecar.com.au).

➡ Both drivers and motorcyclists will need to purchase a Melbourne Pass ($5.50 start-up fee, plus tolls and a 75c vehicle-matching fee per trip) if they're planning on using one of the two toll roads: CityLink, from Tullamarine Airport to the city and eastern suburbs, or EastLink, which runs from Ringwood to Frankston. Pay online or via phone – but pay within three days of using the toll road to avoid a fine.

➡ Driving is on the left-hand side of the road.

➡ The police strictly enforce Victoria's blood alcohol limit of 0.05% with random breath testing (and drug testing) of drivers.

➡ Parking inspectors are particularly vigilant in the city centre. Most of the street parking is metered and it's more likely than not that you'll be fined if you overstay your metered time.

➡ Motorcyclists are allowed to park on the footpath except in some parts of the city centre where there are signs.

Taxi

➡ Melbourne's taxis are metered and require an estimated prepaid fare when hailed between 10pm and 5am (you may need to pay more or get a refund depending on the final fare). Toll charges are added to fares.

➡ Two of the largest taxi companies are:

Silver Top (☑131 008; www.silvertop.com.au).

13 Cabs (☑13 22 27; www.13cabs.com.au).

➡ **Uber** (www.uber. com) also operates in Melbourne.

Essential Information

Discount Cards

The myki Explorer pack ($15; www.ptv.vic.gov.au/tickets/myki/buy-a-myki/myki-explorer/) includes a myki card with one day's unlimited travel on public transport in Melbourne, maps and discounts to attractions.

Emergency & Important Numbers

➡ Australia's country code: ☑61

➡ International access code: ☑0011

➡ Ambulance, fire, police: ☎000

➡ Centres Against Sexual Assault: ☎1800 806 292

➡ Translating & Interpreting Service: ☎131 450

Electricity

Type I
230V/50Hz

Internet Access

➡ Free wi-fi is available at central city spots such as Federation Square, Flinders Street Station, Crown Casino and the State Library.

➡ Free wi-fi is now the norm in most mid-range accommodation, although you sometimes have to pay in both budget and top-end places. Many cafes also offer free wi-fi.

➡ If you're not travelling with your own device, there are plenty of libraries around Melbourne with terminals (though you'll need to bring ID to sign up and prebooking is recommended). Libraries offering access:

City (☎03-9658 9500; 253 Flinders Lane; ◷8am-8pm Mon-Thu, 8am-6pm Fri, 10am-5pm Sat, noon-5pm Sun; ⒭Flinders St).

St Kilda (☎03-9209 6655; http://library.portphillip. vic.gov.au; 150 Carlisle St, St Kilda; ◷10am-8pm Mon-Thu, to 6pm Fri, to 5pm Sat & Sun; ⒢3, 16, 78, ⒭Balaclava).

Prahran (☎03-8290 3344; www.stonnington. vic.gov.au/library/Visit-us/ Prahran-Library; 180 Greville St, Prahran; ◷10am-6pm Mon-Fri, to 1pm Sat; ⒢78, 79, ⒭Prahran).

Money

➡ The Australian dollar is made up of 100 cents. There are 5¢, 10¢, 20¢, 50¢, $1 and $2 coins, and $5, $10, $20, $50 and $100 notes.

➡ Most bank branches have 24-hour ATMs and will accept debit cards linked to international network systems such as Cirrus, Maestro, Visa and MasterCard.

➡ Tipping isn't obligatory in Australia and tips are completely optional, as it's presumed that staff will be paid appropriately by their employers. It's common to tip up to 10% in restaurants, but only if you're completely happy with the service.

Opening Hours

Banks 9.30am-4.30pm Monday to Friday.

Cafes 7am or 8am to around 4pm.

Post Offices 9am-5pm Monday to Friday, to noon on Saturday.

Pubs Roughly noon to midnight, sometimes extended on Friday and Saturday and reduced on Sunday.

Restaurants noon-3pm and 6-10pm; many close on Monday and/or Sunday.

Shops Generally from 9am or 10am to around 5pm to 6pm on weekdays, sometimes staying open to 8pm on Thursday and/or Friday. Reduced hours on Saturday and Sunday.

Public Holidays

Victoria observes the following public holidays:

New Year's Day
1 January

Australia Day
26 January

Labour Day
First or second Monday in March

Good Friday to Easter Monday
In March or April

Anzac Day
25 April

Queen's Birthday
Second Monday in June

Friday before AFL Grand Final
September or October

Melbourne Cup Day
First Tuesday in November

Christmas Day
25 December

Boxing Day
26 December

Safe Travel

There are occasional reports of alcohol-fuelled violence in some parts of Melbourne's city centre

late on weekend nights – particularly in King St.

Smoking

Smoking is forbidden in all enclosed public places.

Telephone

➡ Australia's country code is ☎61.

➡ To dial an international number from within Australia, dial ☎0011 and then the country code.

➡ Mobile-phone numbers start with ☎04.

➡ Many businesses have either a toll-free number (starting with ☎1800) or a number (beginning with ☎1300 or ☎13) that is charged at local call rates; these numbers can't be dialled from outside Australia.

➡ A variety of phonecards can be bought from newsagents and post offices.

➡ Australia's digital network is compatible with GSM 900 and 1800 handsets (used in Europe and New Zealand). Quad-based US phones will also work.

Toilets

Toilets are of the sit-down variety. Free public toilets are scattered around the inner city.

Tourist Information

The **Melbourne Visitor Centre** (☎03-9658 9658; https://whatson.melbourne.vic.gov.au; ⏰9am-6pm; 📶; 🚉Flinders St) at Federation Square has comprehensive information on Melbourne and regional Victoria, resources for mobility-impaired travellers, and a travel desk for accommodation and tour bookings. There are power sockets for recharging phones, too. There's a chance the centre might need to move sometime in 2017 due to construction work nearby.

Travellers with Disabilities

➡ Many of the attractions in Melbourne are accessible for wheelchairs.

➡ Most trains, trams and buses are also accessible by way of ramps and bridging plates.

➡ Pedestrian crossings feature sound cues and accessible buttons. The City of Melbourne has a series of mobility maps available on its website (www.melbourne.vic. gov.au).

➡ **Travellers Aid** centres inside **Flinders Street Station** (☎03-9610 2030; www.travellersaid.org.au; ⏰main concourse; ⏰8am-8pm) and **Southern Cross Station** (☎03-9670 2072; www.travellersaid.org.au; ⏰6.30am-9.30pm) are particularly helpful for those with special needs and offer a variety of facilities for travellers, including baby-change facilities, fully accessible toilets (with ceiling hoist), lounge area, luggage storage and wheelchair hire.

➡ Auslan interpreter service available through **Vicdeaf** (☎TTY 03-9473 1199; www.vicdeaf.com.au).

➡ Download Lonely Planet's free Accessible Travel guide from http://lptravel.to/Accessible Travel

Visas

All visitors to Australia must have a valid passport and visa (New Zealanders receive a 'special category' visa on arrival). Tourist visas are free and valid for three months. The easiest way to obtain a visa is to apply for an Electronic Travel Authority (ETA), which can be done online (www.eta.immi. gov.au) for a service fee of $20 or through your travel agent.

Behind the Scenes

Send Us Your Feedback

We love to hear from travellers – your comments help make our books better. We read every word, and we guarantee that your feedback goes straight to the authors. Visit **lonelyplanet.com/contact** to submit your updates and suggestions.

Note: We may edit, reproduce and incorporate your comments in Lonely Planet products such as guidebooks, websites and digital products, so let us know if you don't want your comments reproduced or your name acknowledged. For a copy of our privacy policy visit lonelyplanet.com/privacy.

Kate's Thanks

Big thanks to Destination Editor, Tasmin Waby, for the opportunity to basically eat and drink my way around Melbourne's best neighbourhoods! Thank you to Caro Cooper for suggestions and being a drinking partner on occasion, and to my partner Trent for all your help and support.

Acknowledgements

Climate map data adapted from Peel MC, Finlayson BL & McMahon TA (2007) 'Updated World Map of the Köppen-Geiger Climate Classification', Hydrology and Earth System Sciences, 11, 1633–44.

Cover photograph: St Kilda Pier at sunset, John W Banagan/Getty ©

Contents photograph: Flinders Street Station, Melbourne, Australia, Ekaterina Kamenetsky/Shutterstock ©

This Book

This 4th edition of Lonely Planet's *Pocket Melbourne* guidebook was curated by Kate Morgan and researched and written by Kate Morgan, Cristian Bonetto and Peter Dragicevich. The previous edition was written by Trent Holden and Kate Morgan. This guidebook was produced by the following:
Destination Editor Tasmin Waby **Product Editor** Rachel Rawling **Senior Cartographer** Julie Sheridan **Book Designer** Gwen Cotter

Assisting Editors Sarah Bailey, Imogen Bannister, Victoria Harrison **Cover Researcher** Campbell McKenzie **Thanks to** Kate Chapman, Sasha Drew, Kate Mathews, Wayne Murphy, Mazzy Prinsep, Kathryn Rowan, Lyahna Spencer

Index

See also separate subindexes for:
Eating p187
Drinking p188
Entertainment p189
Shopping p189

Sights 000
Map Pages **000**

Sights 000
Map Pages p000

Eating

Our Writers

Kate Morgan

Having worked for Lonely Planet for more than a decade, Kate has been fortunate enough to cover plenty of ground working as a travel writer on destinations such as Shanghai, Japan, India, Zimbabwe, the Philippines and Phuket. She has done stints living in London, Paris and Osaka but these days is based in one of her favourite regions in the world – Victoria, Australia. In between travelling the world and writing about it, Kate enjoys spending time at home working as a freelance editor.

Cristian Bonetto

Cristian has contributed to more than 30 Lonely Planet guides to date, spanning cities, regions and countries across four continents, including his homeland, Australia. His musings on travel, food, culture and design have appeared in numerous publications and media outlets around the world. You can follow Cristian's adventures on Instagram (rexcat75) and Twitter (@CristianBonetto).

Peter Dragicevich

After a successful career in niche newspaper and magazine publishing, both in his native New Zealand and in Australia, The last decade Peter has spent writing dozens of guidebooks for Lonely Planet on an oddly disparate collection of countries, all of which he's come to love. He once again calls Auckland, New Zealand his home.

Published by Lonely Planet Global Limited
CRN 554153
4th edition – Nov 2017
ISBN 978 1 78657 156 4
© Lonely Planet 2017 Photographs © as indicated 2017
10 9 8 7 6 5 4 3 2 1
Printed in China

Although the authors and Lonely Planet have taken all reasonable care in preparing this book, we make no warranty about the accuracy or completeness of its content and, to the maximum extent permitted, disclaim all liability arising from its use.